Things You Thought You Knew
(But Don't Count on It!)

Joseph Rosenbloom
Illustrations by Joyce Behr

A Main Street Book

Material in this collection was adapted from
Bananas Don't Grow on Trees: A Guide to Popular Misconceptions
Published by Sterling Publishing Co. Illustrations by Joyce Behr
© 1978 by Joseph Rosenbloom
Polar Bears Like It Hot: A Guide to Popular Misconceptions
Published by Sterling Publishing Co. Illustrations by Joyce Behr
© 1980 by Joseph Rosenbloom

Library of Congress Cataloging-in-Publication Data is available.

1 3 5 7 9 10 8 6 4 2

© 2002 by Sterling Publishing Co., Inc.
Published by Sterling Publishing Co., Inc.
387 Park Avenue South, New York, NY 10016
Distributed in Canada by Sterling Publishing
c/o Canadian Manda Group, One Atlantic Avenue, Suite 105
Toronto, Ontario, Canada M6K 3E7
Distributed in Great Britain by Chrysalis Books
64 Brewery Road, London N7 9NT, England
Distributed in Australia by Capricorn Link (Australia) Pty. Ltd.
P.O. Box 704, Windsor, NSW 2756, Australia
Book design by StarGraphics Studio

Sterling ISBN 1-4027-0409-7

Contents

Chapter 1
People

MIND AND BODY

ALL PEOPLE HAVE THE SAME
NUMBER OF BONES

The normal adult human body has 206 bones, but infants have more bones than adults. The underdeveloped skull of a newborn baby has six gaps or "holes" in it, the largest located in the middle of the top of the head. By the age of two, the skull bones have grown sufficiently to close these "soft spots," and thus the number of bones in the skull is reduced. Also, the last five vertebrae at the lower end of a child's backbone gradually join to form a single bony structure, the sacrum.

In addition, the coccyx or tail bone, located below the sacrum at the very end of the backbone, consists of four tiny bones in some people, but five in others.

A SIMPLE FRACTURE IS A BROKEN BONE WITH ONE BREAK; A COMPOUND FRACTURE HAS MORE THAN ONE BREAK

"Simple" and "compound" are terms that do not refer to the number of broken places on a fractured bone. A simple fracture is one in which the skin has not been broken by the shattered bone. A compound fracture, on the other hand, is one in which the broken bone has been knocked so far out of position that it pierces the overlying skin, bringing the bone in contact with the air and making an infection of the wound possible.

PEOPLE WHO CAN PERFORM FEATS OF GREAT PHYSICAL DEXTERITY ARE DOUBLE-JOINTED

Acrobats and others whose joints seem to be made of rubber have the same number of joints as everyone else. They simply have more flexible ligaments than the rest of us.

THE FUNNY BONE IS A SENSITIVE BONE

The so-called funny bone is not a bone at all. It is the ulnar nerve, which runs in a shallow groove close to the skin on the inside of the elbow. Pressing the ulnar nerve forces it against a nearby bone and causes a shock or a tingling sensation in the forearm and hand.

THE HEART IS ON THE LEFT
SIDE OF THE BODY

Because the aorta, the largest artery leading out of the heart, is on the left side of the body, it is easier to hear or to feel the beat of the heart on the left side, just to the left of the breastbone. This is not exactly the position of the heart, however. A small part of the heart is on the left side of the breastbone and a small portion is on the right side. The bulk of the heart is right in the middle of the chest, slightly tilted.

THE PUPIL OF THE EYE IS A BLACK SPOT

The pupil of the eye only appears to be black; actually it is a transparent hole in the middle of the iris. The pupil looks black because the retina, which lies behind it, is dark in color, and because the illumination inside the eye is small compared to the amount of light outside.

COLD, DAMP WEATHER
CAUSES THE COMMON COLD

Exposure to low temperatures by itself will not bring on a cold. The common cold is caused by viruses. No virus, no cold—no matter how cold and damp the weather. Arctic explorers have reported being free of colds during even the bitterest weather, and colds were almost unknown to Eskimos until the virus was introduced by outsiders.

However, many cold viruses flourish best at low temperatures, and this is why people come down with colds more often in winter than during the summer months. In addition, prolonged exposure to cold, damp weather, like fatigue, can lower one's resistance to cold viruses in the air.

CANCER IS A SPECIFIC DISEASE

Cancer is not a single disease although people speak of it as if it were. It is actually a group of diseases. Over 100 different cancers have been identified. Cancer can occur in any part of the body and has different manifestations. What is common to cancer in all its forms is the uncontrolled and disorderly growth of abnormal cells.

Nor does cancer have a single cause. Although the exact mechanism of cancer is not known, hundreds of separate factors, singly and in combination, have been recognized as possible causes of cancer. Chemicals, radiation, genetic factors, repeated damage to tissues, and viruses, have been suspected in causing certain forms of cancer.

PAIN ON THE RIGHT SIDE
IS A SIGN OF APPENDICITIS

The appendix is a small wormlike structure about 3 inches (7.6 cm) long, attached to the first section of the large intestine. It is normally located on the right side of the body. When the appendix becomes inflamed because of infection, appendicitis results. The infected appendix can be removed surgically in a fairly routine operation. If neglected, however, appendicitis can be fatal.

There is a widespread impression that appendicitis is necessarily associated with a pain or tenderness felt on the right side of the body between the navel and the right hip bone. While the pain is often found where it is expected, in many cases the pain occurs in other parts of the body. It can occur on the left side, anywhere on the lower back, or in the pelvic area. In some instances there may be little or even no perceptible tenderness in the abdomen. In fully half of all appendicitis cases, in fact, the symptoms of pain or tenderness appear elsewhere than on the right side.

If you have a persistent pain in the abdomen, check with your doctor. It is unsafe to assume you cannot have appendicitis because the pain is not on the right side.

THE BLOOD OF THE MOTHER
FLOWS THROUGH THE FETUS

It is not true, as many people suppose, that the blood of the pregnant mother flows through the veins of her baby.

Mother and child are attached by the umbilical chord. The umbilical cord, in turn, is connected to the mother's placenta, a spongy mass rich in blood vessels. The blood vessels in the placenta are from both the mother and her child. However, the two sets of blood vessels are not directly connected in any way. They are kept apart by thin membranes. It is through these membranes that nutriments, oxygen, and wastes are passed by osmosis.

There is normally no actual mingling of the blood of the mother with that of the fetus. The two blood systems are entirely separate.

MAN HAS FIVE SENSES

The idea that we are limited to five senses is possibly due to the fact that we have five obvious organs of sense: eyes, ears, skin, mouth, and nose. However, in addition to the commonly recognized

five senses, scientists now generally speak of four
others. The four additional senses are:

1) the sense of equilibrium, located in the middle
   ear;
2) the kinesthetic sense which keeps us informed
   of what is going on in our muscles, tendons,
   and joints;
3) the sense of heat and cold; and
4) the visceral sense which conveys information
   about internal organ events.

While different scientists classify the senses differently, they are all fairly agreed that we have more than five senses. Whether ESP or other supernatural senses are also to be included in any list of senses is still open to debate.

PERSPIRATION SMELLS

Most of us take frequent baths and make liberal use of deodorants in order to avoid unpleasant perspiration smells. It is commonly supposed that it is the perspiration itself that gives offense.

Perspiration does not give off much of a smell in reality. It is when perspiration comes into contact with bacteria on the skin that it becomes decomposed through bacterial action and begins to emit the characteristic "sweaty" smell we find so objectionable. It is not the perspiration itself, but bacterial action on the perspiration that causes the smell.

The skin of apes and monkeys, by the way, remains dry even in the hottest weather. Profuse perspiration seems to occur in man only. The ability to maintain a steady temperature by means of perspiration seems to be an evolutionary advance of man over the apes and monkeys.

LEARNING CAN TAKE PLACE DURING SLEEP

The idea behind sleep learning is that the subconscious mind is able to absorb new information. Thus, if a phonograph record on which there is a mass of facts is repeatedly played to a person asleep, the person will wake with the facts memorized. Sleep learning would be a boon to those who are too busy during the day or who find it hard to memorize. Sleep learning is a great way to harness the subconscious and make use of time otherwise lost in sleep. Or so they say.

Unfortunately for those who are enthusiastic about sleep learning, research has shown that "sleep learning" takes place only to the extent that the person is awake while the material is being presented. Without awareness, there is no learning.

It might be asserted that sleep learning has validity because a person lying in bed is relaxed and his mind is therefore more open to new material. This is quite another matter, however. Here we are speaking of relaxed learning, not sleep learning. True learning does not take place during true sleep.

A PERSON'S HEAD IS THROWN BACKWARDS IN A HEAD-ON COLLISION

It is widely believed that a person's head will be thrown backwards in any head-on crash. The snapping back of the head is called a "whiplash." Any person who attempted to collect insurance money with the claim that his head was snapped back in a head-on collision would have trouble collecting a dime, however.

The reason stems from a fundamental law of physics; a moving body will continue to move in the same direction unless met by an opposing force. The human body in a forward-moving vehicle will therefore continue to move forward if the vehicle is brought to a sudden halt. Unless restrained by a seat belt, a driver's head may strike the steering wheel or crash into the windshield. Persons in the rear seat may be injured by being suddenly thrown forward. The danger of injury in a forward-moving vehicle comes, not from being suddenly thrown backwards, but forwards.

Only if the vehicle is struck from the rear or the car strikes an object while travelling in reverse, is there a chance of the neck snapping back with sufficient force to be a true whiplash.

WEAK-WILLED PEOPLE ARE MORE EASILY HYPNOTIZED

Since hypnosis is thought to be a matter of one will overpowering another, it is widely believed that weaker people are more readily hypnotized. This is not so. Those who are weak and submissive are not better subjects than those who are strong and intelligent.

Scientists tell us that only one in three or four persons is capable of being hypnotized. The ability to be hypnotized does not depend on sex, intelligence, personality type, age, or anything else so far studied.

A PERSON CAN BE HYPNOTIZED AGAINST HIS WILL

The idea of hypnosis is disturbing to many people. They are under the impression that a hypnotized person is completely subject to the will of the hypnotist. Suggestions implanted by the hypnotist, so it is believed, are executed without hesitation or reservation. The notion that one person can so dominate another is frightening.

In order to be hypnotized, however, a person has to be relaxed and willing. It is not possible to hypnotize a person without his active cooperation. No one can be hypnotized against his will or without his being aware of it.

NERVE IMPULSES TRAVEL AT THE SPEED OF LIGHT

According to the popular view, nerve impulses are electrical in character. Nerve cells may be compared to wires which conduct electric charges. Since electricity flows through a wire at almost the speed of light, 186,282 miles (299,792 km) a second, nerve impulses are also thought to travel at near these speeds. Investigations show this idea to be wrong.

Nerve impulses travel nowhere near the speed of light because they are not merely electrical, but also chemical in nature. Moreover, the nerve cell is not a simple structure comparable to a wire, but a complex one which reacts to the impulses it carries in a variety of physical and chemical ways not entirely understood.

The actual speed at which nerve impulses travel through a nerve depends on the diameter of the nerve fibre. The larger the diameter, the more rapidly the impulse travels. Research conducted in 1943 determined that the fastest messages transmitted by the nervous system reach 265 m.p.h. (366 km p. h.). This is considerably below the speed of sound, let alone the speed of light. As people grow older, not surprisingly, the speed of their nerve impulses slows down.

IT IS NOT POSSIBLE TO GET SUNBURNED ON A CLOUDY DAY

Many people believe they are perfectly safe from sunburn on a cloudy day. This is not the case. It is the ultraviolet rays of the sun that cause sunburn. Actually, 60 to 80 per cent of the amount of ultraviolet rays present on a shining clear day can get through to the human skin on a cloudy day. People are sometimes not aware of this and may occasionally receive severe burns if out too long. This is particularly the case near the water or near white sand where sunlight is reflected. Sunburn can also be caused by reflected glare from ice and snow.

MEN DO NOT LIVE AS LONG AS WOMEN BECAUSE OF THE PACE OF MODERN LIFE

Although women are said to be the weaker sex, their life span is actually six or more years longer than that of men. One reason commonly offered to explain the difference is that the stress of industrialization falls more heavily on men than on women. It is a fact, however, that in all societies around the world, whether industrialized or primitive, women live longer than men. It is, so it would seem, a question of genes and not a matter of style or pace of life.

GIANTS ARE STRONG

Stories about giants are common in the legends of almost all peoples. They are invariably portrayed as evil, barbarous and powerful. The giants in real life are other than strong, however.

Mere tallness is not to be confused with giantism. A tall person is tall for normal reasons, not because of a hormonal problem. True giantism is caused by glandular disorders, most often of the pituitary glands. Giants are susceptible to a wide variety of illnesses and diseases. Many giants are unable to lead normal lives because they are incapacitated in some way.

In contrast to the giants in legends and stories, the giants in real life are generally weak and sickly and have short lives.

FINGERPRINTS ARE OFTEN FOUND ON GUNS

In detective stories the criminal is frequently caught after the police find his fingerprints on a gun. In fact, the police seldom find usable fingerprints on guns for three reasons:

1) When a gun is fired, the force of the recoil moves the gun in the shooter's hand and thus smears the prints.
2) Most guns are oiled frequently, and an oily surface will not make clear impressions.
3) People who shoot guns usually hold them so tightly that fingerprint details are blurred.

SOME PEOPLE DO NOT DREAM

Scientists have determined that when a person dreams his eyes show tiny, rapid eye movements. A rapid eye movement, called REM for short, is a physical indication that dreaming is going on. By using sophisticated measuring devices, and by awakening subjects during REM sleep periods, it has been shown that all people normally dream every night. Even a person who insists that he never dreams will report dreaming if awakened during REM sleep. People who say they never have dreams are simply suppressing their dreams.

There seems to be a real need to dream. Subjects deprived of normal dream periods by being awakened each time they begin to show

REM, show stress and begin to behave abnormally. When subsequently allowed to have REM periods without interruption, the subjects experience more REM sleep than normal. It is as if they had a need to make up for their deprivation.

REM sleep has been observed in many animals. It has been reported among monkeys, dogs, cats, rats, elephants, shrews and opposums. REM has also been detected in some birds and reptiles.

DREAMS ARE OF SHORT DURATION

Most people are under the impression that just as objects and relations are distorted in dreams, so is the sense of time. Dreams which seem to span hours are believed to last but a few seconds. This notion is at odds with what scientists now know about dreams.

When a person has dreams, he has bursts of rapid eye movements. These rapid eye movements are objective indications that a person is dreaming. The first such rapid eye movement, REM for short, generally begins after the onset of sleep and lasts from five to ten minutes. Succeeding REM periods occur about every 90 minutes and last progressively longer. The final dream period often lasts 30 minutes or so. The longest REM period on record lasted two hours and 23 minutes.

Far from being of short duration, dreams actually last substantial periods of time.

A SLEEPWALKER IS ACTING OUT HIS DREAMS

Sleepwalking is commonly regarded as an extension of dreaming. Certain persons will, so the belief goes, rise from bed and act out their dreams if their dreams are intense enough. Sleepwalking is active dreaming, therefore. Not so, say scientists.

Scientists who have studied sleep have shown that the eyes of people who dream flutter slightly. As we have seen, the slight flutter of the eye is

called rapid eye movement, or REM for short. The absence of REM is called NREM, or non-rapid eye movement. To put it simply, when REM is present dreaming is going on, when it is not, as in NREM sleep, dreaming is not going on. It has been shown that sleepwalking takes place entirely during NREM sleep. Sleepwalking is not a dream state, nor is it in any way an extension of dreams.

Persons awakened during a dream know they have been dreaming and are able to recall many details of their dreams. This is quite otherwise in the case of sleepwalking persons. The sleepwalker on being awakened is not aware that he has been sleepwalking and cannot recall any events which took place during his sleepwalking.

MORE MEN THAN WOMEN SNORE

Snoring is generally associated with men. This is not fair to men. Snoring is no respecter of gender. Famous snorers have included George Washington, John and Samuel Adams, Theodore Roosevelt and Winston Churchill. If there are any famous women snorers, they have kept the facts of their snoring a secret.

One out of five persons has a snoring problem. Snoring can affect a person at any age, although it is more widespread among older people. Although more reluctant to admit the problem, women are as likely to snore as men.

Animals also snore. Snoring has been reported among elephants, cows, sheep, cats, dogs, camels, chimpanzees, zebras, buffaloes, and gorillas.

A FAINTING PERSON FALLS BACKWARDS

In motion pictures or on television, a fainting person is typically shown as swooning backwards to the floor or into someone's waiting arms. It may be more dramatic to show a person fainting in this manner, but it is not correct.

The body is so articulated that it is more inclined to fall forward rather than backwards when the muscles relax as they do in a fainting spell. Just relax your body and you will see that you have a tendency to fall forward, not backwards.

DRESS AND GROOMING

ROMANS NEVER WORE TROUSERS

In the popular mind, the Romans wore togas exclusively. This was not entirely true. The Romans also wore trousers called *braccae*.

The "barbarians" living in severe climates commonly wore trousers. The Romans also began to adopt trousers as a practical form of dress while they occupied "barbarian" lands. Although spurned at first as appropriate attire in Rome, the fashion of wearing trousers became commonplace in time. By the 5th century A.D., trousers were regarded as perfectly acceptable attire in Rome itself.

THE KILT WAS INVENTED BY THE SCOTS

The Scottish kilt is by no means the first kilt in the history of men's clothing.

The basic masculine garment of ancient Egypt was a white linen kilt, called the *schenti* by scholars.

It was a rectangular piece of cloth wrapped around the waist and tied in front. The Egyptian *schenti* remained in use throughout the length of ancient Egypt. The Scottish kilt, by comparison, is a relative newcomer. It goes back only to the beginning of the 17th century.

The kilt used by Balkan men is also older than the Scottish kilt, although the date of its origin is not clearly established. The most famous of the Balkan kilts is the kilt worn by Greek men. On feast days and other special occasions, Greek men wear a white pleated kilt known as the *fustanella*. The Evzones, the Greek royal guard, still wear the *fustanella* as part of their full-dress uniform.

The kilt, from what we have seen, is not exclusively Scottish nor was it invented by them.

CUTTING OR SHAVING HAIR
WILL MAKE IT GROW

Cutting or shaving hair will not improve or hasten hair growth. Nor will massaging hair with tonics of any sort cure baldness. Hereditary baldness can sometimes be delayed, but not stopped, by keeping the hair clean and well brushed.

Unless baldness is caused by disease, it is irreversible and final. It is an inherited characteristic transmitted by a sex-influenced gene. If the gene is present, baldness will develop where sufficient testosterone is present. Testosterone is a male hormone that stimulates the growth of body hair but decreases the growth of hair on the scalp.

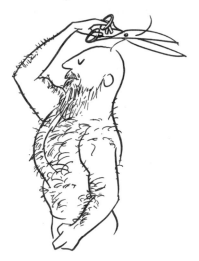

Men with heavy growth of body hair, as a result, tend to lose hair on the scalp at an earlier age than men with scant body hair. Although women carry the genes of hereditary baldness, they do not themselves as a rule become bald, but pass the characteristic on to their sons.

FREQUENT HAIR WASHING CAUSES BALDNESS

Washing one's hair often is not bad for the hair and will not result in baldness as some people think. Hair washed two or three times a week, or even every day, is not affected by washing. So long as the soap is removed with each washing, frequently washing may actually improve the health of hair by helping to get rid of dandruff. Although frequent washing will not cause baldness, by the same token it will not prevent baldness.

As we have seen, baldness, unless caused by disease, is a hereditary condition which cannot be prevented or reversed.

PEOPLE DID NOT BATHE
DURING THE MEDIEVAL PERIOD

Although the expression "cleanliness is next to godliness" is accepted with little question today, it was not always so. During the early medieval period, from the 10th to the 13th centuries, many church authorities taught that refraining from bathing was commendable as a means of doing penance for sins. Uncleanliness became a path to virtue.

It took until the middle of the medieval period for attitudes towards bathing to relax. Medieval kings and noblemen began to bathe at reasonable intervals. As for the common people, opportunities for bathing increased as more and more bathing facilities were built. By the end of the 15th century, public baths were common throughout Europe.

The very lowest point in European cleanliness was not the medieval period, but later. From the 16th to the early 19th centuries, Europeans were among the dirtiest people on earth. For a period of over 200 years, even the wealthy and powerful were filthy. They masked their dirt and smells with cosmetics and perfumes. Nor did the medical profession encourage bathing. They viewed it as unnecessary and harmful. As for the common people, public bathing facilities were rare indeed. Doctors believed that public bathing was a good way to spread disease. It was only by the middle of the 19th century that bathing, public and private, became acceptable once again.

TURBANS ARE TYPICALLY INDIAN

While the turban is still worn in India, it cannot be regarded as typically Indian. The turban is common in a whole string of countries spanning the Near and Middle East. The turban is also seen with more frequency in Africa as more Africans turn Muslim, since the turban is taken as a mark of Muslim affiliation.

Apart from shielding the head against weather, the turban had other uses. The turban originally held weapons—knives, for example. The wearer simply reached into his turban and pulled out a knife in battle. The turban also acted to shield the wearer from blows. The turban could be unwound for a girdle. It could be also used for a pillow at night.

WOODEN SHOES ARE TYPICALLY DUTCH

The wooden shoes of the Dutch are famous. They are called *klompen*. But is it accurate to say that wooden shoes are Dutch?

During the Middle Ages, from about 1,000 A.D. onwards, the peasants of Northern Europe wore carved wooden shoes called *sabots*. These shoes were identical to present-day Dutch wooden shoes. While the Dutch wore *sabots*, in fact, so did the peasants of France, as well as the peasants of Belgium. Thus while the Dutch wore *sabots*, and still do, historically, wooden shoes are Northern European rather than exclusively Dutch.

Interestingly, the word "sabotage" comes from *sabot*. When a peasant wished to avenge himself on his landlord, he trampled his crops with his *sabots*. Sabotage today means to destroy purposefully.

THE BERET IS TYPICALLY FRENCH

The Frenchman is typically pictured as wearing a beret. Some Frenchmen do wear berets, of course, but then again so do some north Italians, some Spaniards, some Yugoslavians, some Irish and others. The beret, in fact, is worn throughout Europe. If the beret is typical of any people, it is of the Basques.

The Basques live in the western part of the Pyrenees Mountains. The lands in which the Basques live are presently divided between France and Spain. The Basques are fiercely independent people whose origin is shrouded in mystery. Even the Basque language is different from any other European tongue.

The beret, called *boina* in Basque, is the national hat of Basque men. No self-respecting Basque would think of being seen in public without his beret. He will seldom remove his *boina*, even to doff it as a greeting.

PANAMA HATS COME FROM PANAMA

The straw hat known as the Panama hat does not come from Panama. The hat actually comes from Ecuador.

FOOD AND DRINK

HOT MEALS ARE MORE NUTRITIOUS

Hot food may be preferred to cold food, but on nutritional grounds alone there is no difference between a hot meal and a cold one. If anything, heating reduces the nutritional value of food by destroying vitamins.

A hot meal may taste better or may warm you on a cold day, but this has nothing to do with the nutritional value of the food.

FOOD IS DIGESTED IN THE STOMACH

The stomach is not the principal organ of digestion, contrary to popular belief. The purpose of the stomach is to store food and reduce it to a pulpy mass by mixing it with gastric juice. The pulpy liquid, called chyme, passes from the stomach to the small intestine. It is in the small intestine that food is broken down into a form which can be absorbed into the bloodstream for the body's use.

Only a tiny fraction of the digestive process takes place in the stomach. Most of the digestive process really takes place in the small intestine.

SEA WATER IS DANGEROUS TO DRINK

Sea water is unpleasant to drink. It is salty and bitter. It is also believed to be highly toxic. Anyone who drinks enough sea water is thought to be courting certain death. No wonder sailors refuse to drink sea water although near death from thirst.

Many lives could be saved, however, if it were realized that sea water is not dangerous, poisonous stuff if taken in moderation. Sea water may not be the most pleasant of thirst quenchers, but it can stave off death. In many instances, sea water can help prolong life until help arrives. Sea water, of course, is not recommended as a normal or steady source of moisture. We are here talking of sea water as an emergency measure intended to help survive until fresh water becomes available.

The notion that sea water is toxic is a dangerous legend. It has cost many lives and should be discarded.

BUTTERMILK HAS A HIGH BUTTERFAT CONTENT

In spite of its name, the exact opposite is the case. Buttermilk is actually milk from which all the butterfat content has been removed.

**HEAVY CREAM WEIGHS
MORE THAN LIGHT CREAM**

Because heavy cream contains more fat, and fat weighs less than an equivalent amount of liquid, heavy cream actually weighs less than light cream. This is why cream rises to the top in fresh (unhomogenized) milk. The misconception arises because the term "heavy" refers to the thickness of heavy cream and not to its weight.

THE BABY RUTH CANDY BAR
IS NAMED AFTER THE BASEBALL PLAYER

The Baby Ruth candy bar was not named after the famous Babe Ruth of baseball but, in fact, after President Grover Cleveland's eldest daughter.

SWALLOWING SEEDS MAY CAUSE APPENDICITIS

If you swallow seeds, grape seeds for example, there is a widespread belief that this is an invitation to appendicitis. Some of the seeds might lodge in the appendix and the presence of the seeds could bring on appendicitis. Is this true?

44

Surgeons report that cases of foreign bodies being found in the appendix are extremely rare. If by some outside chance a seed did lodge in the appendix, it would not of itself cause appendicitis. Appendicitis is not caused by the presence of a foreign body but, instead, is an infection produced by bacteria normally found only in the large intestine.

LEMONS ARE PICKED YELLOW

Oranges are often picked green and color artificially added. Lemons, on the other hand, are thought to be picked yellow without the need for artificial coloration. Virtually all lemons are in fact picked green. Once picked from the tree, the green lemons are placed in curing rooms where temperature and humidity are carefully controlled. The green lemons gradually turn yellow in these curing rooms.

Not only do the lemons turn yellow, but they improve in taste as the result of curing. The lemon is one of those fruits which taste better long after picking rather than fresh from the tree. Lemons may be kept in curing rooms for as long as three months.

GREEN ORANGES ARE IMMATURE

Oranges become orange in color during the cooler winter months. These orange-hued fruits frequently will turn green as warm weather returns. When picked green, the oranges are bleached or dyed artificially before being shipped to market. It is not true, therefore, that green oranges are younger or less mature oranges.

Green oranges may actually be older or more mature oranges than orange oranges.

ORANGES ORIGINATED
IN FLORIDA OR CALIFORNIA

The orange did not originate in Florida or California. Oranges, in fact, originated in Asia and first appeared in southern Europe in the Middle Ages. It was the early Spanish explorers of the 16th century who brought oranges to Florida, and later to California. Every Spanish sailor was required by law to carry 100 orange seeds with him if he was bound for the New World. Oranges did not come to Europe from Florida or California, but the other way around.

PEKOE IS A KIND OF TEA

The term *pekoe* in reference to tea does not mean a type of tea. Pekoe refers, instead, to the size of the tea leaf. Thus, orange pekoe means not a kind of tea but a tea leaf of a certain size.

There are three primary types of tea: black (fully fermented), oolong (partially fermented), and green (unfermented). Other terms used in connection with tea, such as pekoe, orange pekoe, souchong, and fannings, indicate leaf size.

POPCORN IS A MODERN SNACK

Eating popcorn is associated with watching television or the movies. It is therefore thought of as a comparatively recent creation. While the commercial sale of popcorn in large volume did not begin much before this century, the snack is actually much older.

Before the first Europeans arrived, the Indians of North America raised a type of maize suitable for popping and regularly enjoyed popcorn. It was the Indians who introduced the English colonists to the snack. The English colonists first ate popcorn at the famous Thanksgiving dinner held in the autumn of 1621.

Popping results when moisture in the kernel turns into steam. When sufficient pressure builds up, the kernel explodes. The expanded corn often swells up to 30 times its original size on popping.

ENGLISH MUFFINS ARE ENGLISH

English muffins are known only in America. What Americans call English muffins cannot be found in any English shops or bakeries.

CORNED BEEF AND CABBAGE IS AN IRISH DISH

Contrary to popular opinion, corned beef and cabbage is not commonly eaten in Ireland. It became a common food among the early Irish immigrants to the United States because corned beef at five cents a pound was all that many impoverished Irish families could afford at the time.

THE IRISH POTATO ORIGINATED IN IRELAND

The common Irish or white potato, traditionally an important food in Ireland, did not originate there. It is native to the mountainous regions of South America, and today it can still be found growing wild in the uplands of Ecuador and Peru.

When the Spaniards first came to Peru, they found potatoes being cultivated by the South American Indians, who called them *pappas*. The Spaniards brought them back to Spain, where they were called *batates* or *patates*. From Spain, the potato gradually spread throughout much of Europe, reaching England and Ireland by the late 1500s.

While Europeans in general were somewhat reluctant to eat the potato, using it mainly to feed cattle and hogs, the Irish were enthusiastic and soon made it the most important item in their diet. In fact, when the potato crop failed in 1845, the Irish suffered a terrible famine.

FRENCH-FRIED POTATOES ARE FRENCH

The Belgians, not the French, created French-fried potatoes. The Belgians call them *patates frites*, buy them at stands on the street, and carry them away in paper cones.

CHOP SUEY IS A CHINESE DISH

Although it is not certain who first made chop suey, it is thought to have originated in the mining camps in California. It was a sort of pot-luck dish made from whatever ingredients the cook, who was often Chinese, had available. Whether or not this is how the dish came about, chop suey is not known in China and is certainly not Chinese.

THE EARL OF SANDWICH
INVENTED THE SANDWICH

John Montagu, the fourth Earl of Sandwich (1718–1792), is credited with having invented the sandwich. Among the corrupt Earl's vices was an addiction to gambling. It is said that in order to avoid interrupting his card games for meals, he would order a servant to bring him a piece of meat between two slices of bread.

However, long before the Earl of Sandwich gave his name to this familiar food item, the ancient Romans were eating sandwiches of a sort and calling them by the name *offula*, meaning a bit or morsel. And since Roman times, a number of countries have featured sandwiches of one kind or another in their diets.

CHEWING GUM WAS INVENTED IN THE UNITED STATES

Chewing gum is not a recent innovation, nor was it first made in the United States. The ancient Greeks chewed gum from the mastic tree. The Indians of New England chewed a gum made of the resin of spruce trees, and in the early 1800s a commercial chewing gum was marketed in the United States using spruce gum.

Chicle, which was first used by the Mayans and other Central American cultures many centuries ago, was introduced into the United States about 1860 and became the basis of the first modern, popular chewing gum.

BANANAS ARE PICKED GREEN
SO THEY WILL NOT SPOIL IN SHIPMENT

Many fruits are picked while still green to insure that they do not become too ripe during shipment and storage—but not bananas.

Bananas will not ripen properly if left on the banana plant. Even those intended to be eaten locally are picked green. If allowed to ripen on the plant, bananas lose some of their flavor, their skins sometimes break open and bacteria and insects enter.

SPICES WERE VALUED IN THE MIDDLE AGES
BECAUSE THEY FLAVORED AND PRESERVED FOOD

As everyone knows, the search for a short route to the Far East and its spices led to the discovery and exploration of the New World. Spices, and pepper in particular, were terribly costly by the time they reached Europe because of the long haul over thousands of miles, across deserts, mountains and rivers. Nature took a terrible toll of caravans carrying spices, which were also often attacked by bands of robbers. Vast

wealth and power awaited the discoverers of a new and better route to the East.

What is not commonly known is that spices were not used primarily to add flavor to and preserve food. They were sought in far-away lands and highly valued because of their use in the preparation of various medicines.

THE SOFT DRINK IS AN AMERICAN INVENTION

The flavored carbonated water drink has been developed to a greater degree in the United States than in any other country, but it was more or less invented by Joseph Priestley (1733–1804) when the great English scientist made the first glass of carbonated water in 1767.

Some 40 years later, a Philadelphia druggist added fruit flavors to Priestley's fizzing water to make the first carbonated beverage. The drink was enormously popular and soon many competing products in all colors and flavors appeared.

ICE CREAM COOLS YOU OFF

Ice cream tastes good and feels cold, but it does not cool you, although you may imagine that it does after eating some on a hot day. Ice cream is so rich in fat and so full of calories that it ultimately makes the human body warmer, not cooler.

ICE CREAM ORIGINATED IN THE UNITED STATES

To many people, ice cream seems as American as apple pie. Although the United States does lead all other countries in the total amount of ice cream produced, ice cream is not an American creation.

Ice cream seems to have developed from flavored ice dishes that were eaten in ancient times. It is known that wines and fruit juices were added to snow in the court of the Roman emperor Nero in the 1st century A.D.

After the fall of Rome, ice cream disappeared from Europe and was not reintroduced until the 13th century, when Marco Polo, the great Venetian explorer, brought back from the Orient recipes for a more advanced dish containing milk as the main ingredient. The art of making ice cream then spread throughout Europe, and the early English settlers introduced ice cream into the New World in the 1600s.

Chapter 2
History

THE UNITED STATES

THE PILGRIMS LANDED AT PLYMOUTH ROCK

Contrary to the widely held belief, the Pilgrims did not land at Plymouth Rock when they first arrived in the New World in 1620.

The facts are that the Pilgrims on the *Mayflower* sighted Cape Cod on November 19, 1620. Their ship dropped anchor on November 21 at what is now Provincetown at the tip of Cape Cod. They took on water and supplies and mended their small dinghy, which they used to explore the coast. It was a month later, on December 21, that Plymouth Harbor was visited by the Pilgrims and found suitable for a settlement. Five days later, the *Mayflower* was anchored at Plymouth.

Not only did the Pilgrims not land first at Plymouth, but, according to historical evidence, they did not land at Plymouth Rock when they got there. The earliest Pilgrim records make no mention of Plymouth Rock. Historians now regard the story of Plymouth Rock as legendary rather than factual.

THE FIRST AMERICAN SETTLERS
LIVED IN LOG CABINS

The first settlers in America did not live in primitive log cabins. John Smith, Governor Bradford, the Founding Fathers—none lived in log cabins.

After living in temporary shelters on first arriving in the New World, the early English settlers promptly set about constructing frame or brick houses, not log cabins.

Log cabins became common only much later in the Western frontier regions, far from the settled Eastern seaboard. For example, Abraham Lincoln was born in a log cabin on the Kentucky frontier in 1809.

The many pictures showing Puritans returning to their log cabins after sharing a Thanksgiving dinner with the Indians, are based on imagination, not fact.

WITCHES WERE BURNED IN SALEM

It is widely and mistakenly believed that people accused of being witches were burned in Salem, Massachusetts, in the late 17th century. Actually, the method of execution for those convicted of witchcraft in Salem was by hanging and, on at least one occasion, by pressing with heavy stones.

In Salem, 19 persons—13 women and 6 men—were hanged. While the witch hunt fever was one of the darker pages in American history, the situation was far worse in Europe, where thousands of persons believed to be witches were burned to death and beheaded during the fifteenth, sixteenth and seventeenth centuries.

THE BOSTON TEA PARTY WAS CAUSED BY THE HIGH PRICE OF TEA

The Boston Tea Party, December 16, 1773, is regarded by historians as the opening incident in the train of events leading to the American Revolution. The reason for the dumping of tea in Boston Harbor was not, as many people suppose, because the price of tea was excessive. The price of tea was actually cheaper in America than it was in England.

In order to bolster the financially troubled East India Tea Company, Parliament granted the Company the exclusive right to supply tea to America. All middlemen were cut out and all ordinary import duties were suspended. As a result, the tea reaching American shores was quite cheap. At King George's insistence, however, and in spite of strenuous objections by many of his advisors, a modest threepence tax was added to each pound of tea imported. Even with this tax added, the cost of tea was still cheaper in New York than in London.

King George viewed the modest tax as a question of principle. The failure to collect what was really little more than a token tax, he feared, might weaken the power of the Crown to tax in the future. The right of the Crown to tax as it saw fit was to be maintained at any cost. The American patriots felt differently. Those, they said, who had to pay taxes were entitled to some say in how they were to be taxed. The lines for a confrontation over the principle of taxation were being drawn.

Thus it was not the price of tea, but an entirely different issue, that led to the Boston Tea Party and ultimately to the American Revolution.

MOST AMERICANS SUPPORTED
THE REVOLUTIONARY WAR

During the American Revolution, the Loyalists (or Tories) were a rather substantial portion of the population. These people thought the colonies should remain under British rule, and so opposition to the revolution was strong.

No less a person than John Adams (1735-1826), the second U.S. President, estimated the Loyalists to be a third of the population, and believed another third were uncommitted to either side in the conflict.

The number of Loyalists varied from colony to colony, and from time to time. Many people simply sided with the army that was stationed nearest their community, or the one that appeared to be winning. As many as 100,000 Loyalists out of a total population of 2,500,000 left the colonies during the Revolution, primarily to settle in Canada. At one time during a period when George Washington had fewer than 10,000 men under his command, there were as many as 8,000 Loyalists serving with the British.

Contrary to popular belief, then, a large number of Americans, perhaps even a majority, disagreed completely or in part with the aims of the revolution, and remained loyal to England.

GEORGE WASHINGTON NEVER SERVED WITH THE BRITISH

Because George Washington is identified as the father of his country and the leader of its army during the American Revolution, few people realize that he first served in the British army.

George Washington, in fact, served for nearly six years with the British during the French and Indian War, advancing to the rank of full colonel. He later put this military experience to use *against* England. Without this military background and training in leadership under the British, Washington might not have led the American Revolution to a successful conclusion.

FEW FOREIGN TROOPS FOUGHT IN THE AMERICAN REVOLUTION

Most people are aware that the Hessians fought on the British side during the American War of Independence. Not many know the full extent of the Hessian military contribution. Fewer still are aware of the importance of French forces to the successful outcome of the war.

To increase the strength of their army, the British bought the services of soldiers from various petty German rulers. (The employment of mercenaries, or foreign soldiers who fought for pay, was more common then than it is today.) Because so many of the hired troops came from Hesse, they came to be known as Hessians. Far from being an insignificant minority, a total of about 30,000 Hessians served alongside the British. The British Army, by comparison, probably totaled no more than 42,000 effectives at any time during the war, and far fewer most of the time. The Hessian military involvement on the British side was therefore greater than is commonly realized.

The French not only advanced money to the Americans (20,000,000 francs—a huge sum in those days), but also furnished substantial naval and land forces. The French role became especially important in the later phases of the war. The French contribution included all the officers and men of 62 naval vessels as well as 13 regiments. The naval forces were particularly important in the war, since the young American Navy was no match for the British. It is estimated that a total of 47,000 French soldiers and sailors participated in the war on the American side.

While it is true that the French forces came and went, their number was still substantial compared to the purely American forces. In August 1776, Washington had about 20,000 men under his command. This was the largest, but also the rawest, American force ever assembled during the war. After Valley Forge, when the number of Americans had dwindled to a mere 4,000 troops, Washington was lucky to have more than 10,000 regulars available at any one time on all fronts. Probably no more than a total of 100,000 American men bore arms. This number includes repeated enlistments since men did not usually serve for the entire course of the war but enlisted two, three, or more times. Perhaps half of the 100,000 served in the army and the rest in the various state militias. We would have to conclude from these figures that the French military involvement of 47,000 men was substantial.

In two major battles, French forces actually exceeded the American. One was the Battle of Savannah (October 9, 1779). Benjamin Lincoln (1733–1810), the American general in command of the allied forces, had a total of 5,000 men at his disposal. His troops consisted of 3,500 French and 1,500 Americans. Casualties were 640 French killed or wounded and 450 Americans.

The second battle was the final and decisive battle of the war, the Battle of Yorktown (September 28–October 19, 1781). The total number of forces serving under Washington at Yorktown amounted to 40,000 men. Of this number 31,000 were French and 9,000 were American. Most of the French were naval personnel, only 7,000 serving on land. The 16,000 combined American and French soldiers far outnumbered the 7,000 British under Lord Cornwallis (1738–1805). After heavy losses made further resistance all but impossible, Lord Cornwallis sought to save his besieged army by escaping to the sea. A British fleet of 19 ships tried to break through the blockade thrown up by 28 French ships. The British could not punch their way through. Outnumbered on land and bottled up by French ships, Lord Cornwallis agreed to surrender. With the defeat of Cornwallis, the war was over for all practical purposes. The French role was decisively important.

PAUL REVERE MADE
HIS FAMOUS RIDE ALONE

On the night of April 18, 1775, Paul Revere (1735-1818) set out on horseback to warn the people of the Massachusetts countryside that the British troops would be advancing the next morning. He hoped to reach Lexington and warn John Hancock and Samuel Adams, and then push on to Concord to rouse the other citizens.

On that famous night, not one but two men set out from Boston to warn the patriots. One was Paul Revere, the subject of Longfellow's famous poem; the other was William Dawes. Dawes went by way of Boston Neck and Revere by way of Charlestown. Revere arrived in Lexington about half an hour before Dawes. Hancock and Adams, being warned, fled. Then, before Revere and Dawes continued to Concord, a third man, Samuel Prescott, joined them.

Revere, however, was captured by a British patrol, and Dawes, though he escaped, had to turn back. Only Prescott was able to get past British lines and complete Paul Revere's midnight ride to Concord, which enabled the Minutemen there to assemble and to conceal most of the supplies before the British arrived.

While Paul Revere's role as a great American patriot should not be minimized, it should also be recognized that he had two other riders to help him on that memorable midnight ride.

THE BATTLE OF BUNKER HILL WAS FOUGHT ON BUNKER HILL

The Battle of Bunker Hill was fought not on Bunker Hill, but on nearby Breed's Hill on June 17, 1775. This is why the monument commemorating the Battle of Bunker Hill is actually located on Breed's Hill.

Moreover, the Battle of Bennington, an important early victory of the American forces during the American Revolution, was not fought in Bennington, Vermont; it took place near Walloomsac, New York, 4 miles (6.4 km) northwest of Bennington, on August 16, 1777. The battle was so named because it happened after British troops were sent by General John Burgoyne to Bennington to seize desperately needed supplies stored there. Before they could reach Bennington, however, the 1,400 British and Hessian troops were met near Walloomsac and defeated by 2,600 untrained American militia under General John Stark.

THE LIBERTY BELL CRACKED WHEN
IT WAS RUNG ON JULY 8, 1776

The Liberty Bell in Independence Hall in Philadelphia was rung on July 8, 1776 to proclaim the Declaration of Independence, but it did not crack on this occasion. It was on July 8, 1835 that the famous bell cracked during a funeral procession carrying the body of Chief Justice John Marshall

through Philadelphia. The bell, after repair, was often used again, but in 1846, while being rung on the occasion of George Washington's birthday, it suddenly cracked again. This time the damage could not be repaired, and the bell was taken down and put on permanent display.

THE AMERICAN DOLLAR WAS THE PRINCIPAL CURRENCY AFTER THE REVOLUTION

The United States dollar was not the principal coin of the young American republic. The Spanish dollar had been the predominant coin in the early colonial period and continued to be so even after the American Revolution. The exchange rate for other currencies was commonly expressed in terms of the Spanish dollar.

It was not until 1857 that foreign coins, including the Spanish dollar, were declared not to be legal tender.

ALL U.S. PRESIDENTS WERE NATURAL-BORN CITIZENS

Because all modern Presidents were born citizens of the United States, it is widely assumed that all Presidents were natural-born citizens. Actually, the first seven Presidents were not born United States citizens, but British subjects. When these Presidents were born, to put it simply, there was no such thing as the United States. Martin Van Buren (1837–1841), the eighth President, was the first United States President to have been born an American citizen.

The United States Constitution requires that: "No person except a natural born Citizen, or a Citizen of the United States, shall be eligible to the Office of President...." Once the Constitution was ratified, unless they declined citizenship (which many Loyalists did), all former British subjects automatically became citizens of the United States. The first seven Presidents were thus granted citizenship and became eligible for the office.

"THE STAR-SPANGLED BANNER" HAS
ALWAYS BEEN THE NATIONAL ANTHEM
OF THE UNITED STATES

Not so. *The Star-Spangled Banner* was written by Francis Scott Key (1779–1843) during the War of 1812 and thereafter was often played on patriotic occasions, but it did not become the official national anthem until almost 120 years later, on March 3, 1931, when the Congress of the United States passed the act which made the song the nation's anthem.

Furthermore, it is not widely known that Francis Scott Key wrote only the words of the song. Ironically, the tune of *The Star-Spangled Banner* was taken from *To Anacreon in Heaven*, an English song!

THE STORY OF JOHNNY APPLESEED
IS PURE LEGEND

The Johnny Appleseed legend concerns an American pioneer and folk hero who roamed the American frontier distributing apple seeds and planting small orchards. This is one of those rare instances in which legend is based on fact.

The real Johnny Appleseed was John Chapman, born September 26, 1774 in Leominster, Mass. For 50 years John Chapman, or Johnny Appleseed, wandered up and down the Ohio Valley from the Allegheny River to the Saint Mary's River, planting apple seeds and small orchards. John Chapman was not only important for the spread of fruit growing in the young nation, but also because he acted as a frontier Paul Revere. He warned isolated frontier settlements of possible Indian attacks during the War of 1812.

John Chapman died on March 10, 1845 in Allen County in northeastern Indiana.

BASEBALL WAS INVENTED IN THE UNITED STATES BY ABNER DOUBLEDAY

Baseball is regarded as the American national sport, and legend has it that Abner Doubleday created the game and its rules in 1839 in Cooperstown, New York. However, the term "baseball" was in use a full century before Doubleday is said to have coined it. Moreover, there is strong evidence that two English games, cricket and rounders, were the real ancestors of baseball.

Rounders was introduced into the American colonies from England in the 18th century.

As for Doubleday's role in the creation of baseball, it is overshadowed by the contribution made by Alexander Cartwright. It was Cartwright, not Doubleday, who established many of the rules of modern baseball in 1845. He drew a diagram of a ball field with 90-foot (27.4-m) baselines, and had the batter stand at home plate rather than in a separate batter's box away from home plate. He made the infield diamond-shaped, reduced the number of bases from 5 to 4, and introduced flat bases instead of stakes. He also eliminated the rule permitting players to make an "out" by hitting a baserunner on the opposing team with the ball whenever he was not touching the base (a rule Abner Doubleday used in his games). While other rules he devised were different from those in present use, Cartwright must be credited with creating most of the important features of modern baseball.

Cartwright also formed the first baseball club, the New York Knickerbockers, and his rules were used in the first recorded game on June 19, 1846, when the Knickerbockers played in Hoboken, New Jersey.

THE FIRST BATTLE OF IRONCLAD SHIPS WAS BETWEEN THE *MONITOR* AND THE *MERRIMACK*

It is widely supposed that the first battle of armored ships, which took place on March 9, 1862, in Hampton Roads, Virginia, during the American Civil War, was fought between the *Monitor* (North) and the *Merrimack* (South). The battle actually involved the *Monitor* and the *Virginia*.

The North built the *Merrimack* as a United States Navy frigate in 1856, five years before the outbreak of the war. When the war began, the *Merrimack* was in the Norfolk (Virginia) Navy Yard in Confederate territory. To prevent the ship from falling into Confederate hands, it was sunk by retreating Union forces. Later, Confederate engineers raised the ship and converted it into an ironclad vessel. It was this salvaged, redesigned version of the *Merrimack*, renamed the *Virginia*, that fought with the *Monitor*.

ALEXANDER GRAHAM BELL INVENTED
THE TELEPHONE

Alexander Graham Bell (1847–1922) did not invent the telephone alone. That distinction should be shared with another American, Elisha Gray (1835–1901).

Elisha Gray came up with a practical design for the telephone at the same time as Alexandar Graham Bell. Both men, in fact, applied to the U.S. Patent Office on the same day, February 14, 1876, within two hours of each other. Neither was aware at the time that the other had also applied for a patent.

At the time the two patents were applied for, neither Gray nor Bell had undertaken to transmit speech. It would appear that Gray's design was superior. The design submitted to the U.S. Patent Office by Gray would have worked, while that described in Bell's patent would not have. In any case, Gray did not press as hard as he might have to further his claim as the inventor of the telephone. He had either thought he had already lost the race to Bell, or he did not sufficiently appreciate the necessity of going into immediate commercial production.

Alexander Graham Bell, on the other hand, let nothing stand in his way. He pushed on both to perfect his design and get it into commercial production. By the time Gray thought of fighting Bell's claim to being the exclusive inventor of the telephone, it was too late. After years of wrangling in the courts, Bell was legally named the inventor of the telephone.

The court decision is viewed by many today as being unfair and one-sided. It failed to take into account Gray's contribution to the development of the telephone. His work was easily as significant as Bell's, and Elisha Gray should at least have been acknowledged as the co-inventor of the telephone.

In 1872, Elisha Gray founded the Western Electric Company, the parent firm of the present Western Electric Company.

EDISON INVENTED THE LIGHT BULB

Thomas Alva Edison (1847–1931) is unfairly credited with being the sole inventor of the light bulb. Sir Joseph Swan (1828–1914), English chemist and inventor, began to work on an incandescent lamp beginning in 1848. The lamps he made gave feeble light and burned out quickly for lack of a good vacuum and an adequate source of current. The technology of the period was not advanced enough to meet the technical problems involved, and he ceased his experiments by 1860.

Some years later, Sir Joseph Swan resumed working on the light bulb. By 1878, he had developed a satisfactory design using a carbon filament in an evacuated glass tube. Edison came up with an identical solution, but one year later.

Edison is associated with the light bulb not because he was the first to come up with a workable light bulb, but because his activities led to the development of power lines and other equipment needed to make the light bulb part of a practical lighting system.

THE SPANIARDS SANK THE BATTLESHIP "MAINE"

An event that helped bring on the Spanish-American War was the sinking of the U.S.S. *Maine* in the harbor of Havana, Cuba, on the night of February 15, 1898. The explosion caused the death of 2 officers and 258 members of the crew.

When news of the sinking reached American shores, the Spaniards were immediately accused of sinking the battleship, and the nation was incited to outrage, particularly by conservative newspapers. "Remember the Maine!" became the war cry.

Actually, the cause of the sinking was never determined. It is still not known precisely what caused the explosion, or whether it came from inside or outside the ship.

As an excuse for going to war with Spain, the sinking of the *Maine* was a poor one.

NEW YORK HAS ALWAYS BEEN THE LARGEST CITY IN AMERICA

Philadelphia, not New York City, was the largest city in the United States during the early years of the young republic.

In the census of 1790, Philadelphia ranked first, with 42,000 people. New York was second with 32,000. In the censuses of 1800 and 1810, Philadelphia continued to rank first. It was not until the census of 1820 that New York City overtook Philadelphia. New York's population in 1820 was 123,706; Philadelphia's was 119,325. The difference between the two cities was not so large that Philadelphia might not hope to recover first place. With the opening of the Erie Canal in 1825, however, future rivalry was all but impossible, since New York thus became the main point of departure for the Midwest.

By 1840, New York City has a population of 312,710, while Philadelphia had 100,000 fewer.

THE LARGEST AMERICAN CITY
IN AREA IS LOS ANGELES

Los Angeles is famed for its spread-out geography and its many sections connected by what seem to be endless freeways. However, Los Angeles is only second in size; Jacksonville, Florida, far smaller in population, is the largest American city in physical size. Jacksonville has an area of 840 square miles (2,184 square km), while Los Angeles has a mere 464 square miles (1,206 square km).

HOLLYWOOD IS A CITY IN CALIFORNIA

Although more than a dozen states have towns or villages name Hollywood, there is at present no town or city in California bearing that name.

An area that is now part of Los Angeles was settled in the 1880s and was named Hollywood in 1887 by Mrs. Horace H. Wilcox, wife of an early developer. Hollywood was incorporated as a city in 1903. In 1910, the residents voted to become part of Los Angeles. Hollywood is presently a district in the city of Los Angeles, situated about 8 miles (12 km) north of the Los Angeles Civic Center. Although famous as the heart of the motion picture industry. Hollywood is largely a residential community.

CHICAGO IS THE WINDIEST CITY IN THE UNITED STATES

Chicago has a reputation for being a particularly windy place, and is well known as "the windy city." But is this reputation deserved? Surprisingly, Chicago ranks 16th on the list of windiest U.S. cities. According to the U.S. Weather Bureau, Boston (Massachusetts), Des Moines (Iowa), Omaha (Nebraska) and Dallas (Texas), to name but a few, are far windier.

THE UNITED STATES IS A NATION OF BIG CITIES

Contrary to popular belief, the United States is not a nation of big cities. The percentage of people who live in large cities has remained unchanged since 1910. In that year, 9.2 per cent of the population of the United States lived in cities of 1,000,000 or over. In 1970, the figure remained the same: 9.2 per cent of the population lived in cities of a population of 1,000,000 or over. Only the percentage of persons living in small cities, those cities with populations from 10,000 to 100,000 grew between 1910 and 1970.

Nor is the United States an urban nation. Beginning with the 1970 census, the United States became a suburban nation. According to the census of 1970, 75,600,000 persons lived in the suburbs, 63,200,000 in the rural areas, but only 63,800,000 in the central cities. From these figures we must conclude that only 21.5 per cent of Americans live in central cities. The remainder live in the suburbs or in rural areas. The suburbanization of America shows every sign of continuing at the expense of the large cities.

POSTAL RATES HAVE NEVER BEEN HIGHER

Because of recent dramatic increases in postal rates, it is commonly supposed that postal rates have never been higher. This is not so.

Early postal rates depended on how far the letter was to be sent. In 1824, for example, the U.S. postal service charged 6 cents for carrying a "single" letter 36 miles (58 km) or less. For more than 36 miles (58 km) and less than 80 miles (129 km), the charge was 10 cents. From 80 miles (129 km) to 150 miles (242 km) the charge was $12^{1}/_{2}$ cents, and from 150 miles (242 km) to 400 miles (644 km), $18^{1}/_{2}$ cents. For any distance over 400 miles (644 km), the rate was 25 cents. By a "single" letter was meant a letter containing a single piece of paper. When two pieces of paper were enclosed, the charge was doubled; when three pieces of paper were enclosed, the rate was tripled, and so on.

While it may not make us any more willing to pay today's postal rates, people in the past did pay more. Also, the cent in those days was worth several times ours. Today's postal rates may be bargains after all.

THE CANDIDATE WITH THE MOST VOTES IS ELECTED PRESIDENT

It is not true that the candidate receiving the most votes is automatically elected President of the United States. It is the Electoral College rather than the direct popular vote which determines who becomes President. In four presidential campaigns the winning candidate actually received fewer votes from the members of the Electoral College. The four elections occurred in 1824, 1876, 1888, and 2002.

YEAR	CANDIDATES	PERCENTAGE OF POPULAR VOTE
1824	Andrew Jackson	43.1
	John Quincy Adams*	30.5
1872	Samuel Tilden	51.5
	Rutherford B. Hayes*	48.5
1888	Grover Cleveland	48.6
	Benjamin Harrison*	47.9
2002	Albert Gore, Jr.	48.4
	George W. Bush*	47.9

*Winner of election

THE WORLD

THE ROMANS USED CHARIOTS IN WARFARE

The chariot was first used in war by the Sumerians about 2000 B.C. The Egyptians later made good use of chariots in their battles. The Romans also saw the value of the chariot. The Romans reserved the chariot for processions and racing, however. They developed a passion for chariot races, organized chariot teams, and ran as many as 20 races a day.

But the Romans never used chariots in battle as many people believe.

JULIUS CAESAR WAS A ROMAN EMPEROR

Julius Caesar (100–44 B.C.) was a famous Roman general, statesman, orator and writer. He was consul five times and held the title of dictator, but he was never emperor. In Julius Caesar's time, Rome was a republic; the Roman Empire was not founded until 17 years after Caesar was murdered, when Augustus became the first Roman emperor.

CLEOPATRA WAS AN EGYPTIAN

Cleopatra (69–30 B.C.) may have been the Queen of Egypt, but she was not an Egyptian. She was part Macedonian, part Greek and part Iranian.

In Egyptian history, Cleopatra is really not very important. She was the last of the corrupt and greedy Ptolemaic rulers, and her importance lies mainly in her association with Julius Caesar and Mark Antony.

NERO FIDDLED WHILE ROME BURNED

The Roman emperor Nero (37 A.D.–68 A.D.) is infamous as a cruel and evil ruler. He was also an amateur musician who took pride in his musical abilities. It is a widely held belief that this foul emperor played the fiddle while two-thirds of Rome was destroyed by a fire that raged for nine days in 64 A.D.

In fact, Nero could not have played the fiddle while Rome burned. The violin and similar instruments were not invented until the 16th century. If Nero played any instrument at all while Rome burned, it was probably the small harp-like instrument called a lyre.

POMPEII WAS DESTROYED BY MOLTEN LAVA

The common notion that Pompeii was destroyed by molten lava is wrong. It was not the lava but the fumes and ashes which killed many of Pompeii's inhabitants and buried the city.

Actually, there were two disasters which struck Pompeii. In 63 A.D., a great earthquake nearly destroyed it. The occupants of Pompeii began to rebuild the city, but during the rebuilding, in 79 A.D., Mount Vesuvius, a nearby volcano, erupted in a huge explosion. Pompeii and the nearby cities of Herculaneum and Stabiae were buried under ashes.

Had Pompeii been buried under molten lava, it could not have been so readily unearthed centuries later and so much of it so wonderfully preserved. Visiting Pompeii to see the remains of the city is now popular with tourists.

It is not known how many of Pompeii's 20,000 to 22,000 inhabitants perished during the eruption.

THE BAGPIPE ORIGINATED IN SCOTLAND

The bagpipe dates back to early civilization. It probably originated in the Middle East, perhaps in Persia, and was introduced to Europe and the British Isles by the Romans. This musical instrument is most popular in Scotland, but it exists in one form or another in Italy, France, Ireland, Germany, the Balkans and even Scandinavia.

ARABIC NUMERALS WERE INVENTED BY THE ARABS

Contrary to popular belief, Arabic numerals were not invented by the Arabs. They actually originated in India.

Symbols resembling Arabic numerals are found in Indian caves dating as far back as the 3rd and 4th centuries A.D. The early Indian mathematicians made important contributions to the development of arithmetic and algebra because they were familiar with Arabic numerals and their use. Arab traders and scholars subsequently carried these numerals to the Moslem world. The Arabs, or Moors, of North Africa finally introduced the numerals to Europe in the 10th century, just about the time Europe was beginning to emerge from the Dark Ages.

Arabic numerals are called such not because they were invented by the Arabs but because it was the Arabs who brought them to Europe from India.

SANTA CLAUS WAS NOT A REAL PERSON

People who say that Santa Claus has no basis in fact are wrong. The beloved image of the fat, jolly, bearded man in a red suit who brings gifts at Christmastime is based on a person who really lived.

St. Nicholas, long considered the patron saint of children, merchants and sailors, was a 4th cen-

tury Christian bishop in the Near East. He
became the guardian saint of sailors in the 11th
century and thereafter European seamen built
many churches in his honor. It became the custom of choir boys of these churches to go around
seeking small gifts on December 6th, the supposed birthday of the saint. The custom of giving
gifts on St. Nicholas' Day spread throughout
Europe, and eventually the celebration became
associated with Christmas.

The early Dutch settlers brought with them to America the idea of the kindly, gift-giving St. Nicholas and the custom became popular among the colonists there. Thus St. Nicholas (or Santa Claus, as he was called) became the cherished symbol of Christmas in America as well.

A MEDIEVAL KNIGHT IN ARMOR WAS HELPLESS

A persistent but mistaken belief about medieval life is that the fully dressed knight was a prisoner in his own armor. It is thought that the suit of armor was so heavy and rigid that the knight could not get on or off his horse without assistance, and could move his arms and legs only slightly.

The facts are otherwise. A suit of armor was well fitted and weighed only 50 to 55 pounds (22.7 kg to 24.9 kg), about as much as a fully equipped modern soldier's gear. A knight could move around easily, mount and dismount without help, climb ladders, and perform as readily as any other medieval soldier.

KING ARTHUR WAS A KING

Whether such a person as King Arthur actually existed in Britain during the 6th century A.D. is a matter of some debate among historians. Such evidence as is available, however, suggests that King Arthur was not a king. In all probability, he was not even British.

The earliest Welsh historian, Gildas, about 510 A.D., makes no mention of King Arthur. Nennius, writing more than two centuries later, about 800, makes reference to Arthur but not as king. The first continuous account of King Arthur's career was written three centuries later in 1137 by Geoffrey of Monmouth in his *History of the Kings of England*. Other versions of the story of King

Arthur would be fashioned by poets and writers in subsequent centuries right up to the present time. The resulting body of writings is known collectively as the Arthurian Romances. The Arthurian Romances are essentially literary, not historical, writings.

From available historical evidence we must conclude that King Arthur was not a king. He was a hired military leader or general engaged by the numerous petty British kings and chieftains to coordinate their forces against the Germanic invaders who were threatening to take over the entire country. Nennius refers to Arthur as *dux bellorum*, a Roman title which may be translated as "generalissimo" or "commander-in-chief." King Arthur was neither King of Great Britain, nor king of anything else for that matter.

It is probable that Arthur was not British, but was a descendant of the Romans who had invaded Britain in the 1st century and remained up until the 4th century. Arthur may have been a Roman or, at the very least, of mixed Roman-British ancestry.

WILLIAM TELL WAS A REAL PERSON

William Tell, the symbol of Swiss freedom against tyranny and foreign domination, was a legendary rather than a real person.

According to folk tales and legends, an Austrian official by the name of Gessler ruled the Swiss district of Uri during the 14th century. He ruled with an iron hand. Gessler ordered the people of Uri to pay homage to a cap hung in the square of the village of Altdorf. The cap symbolized Austrian domination over the Swiss. The leader of Swiss opposition to the Austrians was William Tell, according to legend.

Gessler was infuriated by William Tell's defiance. In order to make an example of him, he ordered Tell to take a bow and arrow and shoot an apple from the top of his son's head. Thus goodness triumphed over evil, and freedom over tyranny. William Tell is said to have later taken the life of Gessler. The Swiss were thus free of foreign domination.

The earliest version of the Tell legend appeared in the 15th century and has inspired plays and operas. However, in spite of efforts by scholars to substantiate the existence of such a person, no evidence has been uncovered to show that a William Tell existed in 14th-century Switzerland.

FERDINAND MAGELLAN WAS THE FIRST TO SAIL AROUND THE WORLD

Many people are under the impression that Ferdinand Magellan (1480?–1521) was the first to circumnavigate the earth, but this is not true.

Magellan set sail from Spain on September 20, 1519. He crossed the Atlantic, reached South America and sailed southwards down the coast until he rounded the southern tip along a route now called the Strait of Magellan. He then crossed the Pacific and reached the Philippines where he was killed on the island of Mactan on April 27, 1521.

The voyage back to Spain was completed by the ship Victoria under the command of Juan Sebastian del Cano. Magellan, therefore, did not live to complete the circumnavigation of the world. The first commanding navigator to actually accomplish this feat was the English admiral Sir Francis Drake (1543–1596).

THE AZTECS AND INCAS WERE LARGELY DESTROYED BY SPANISH ARMS

The Spanish military campaigns brought considerable death and destruction to the Aztecs and Incas. However, far more damaging to these great civilizations were the diseases carried to the New World by the Spaniards. The Aztecs and Incas, having no immunity to the germs common in Spain, suffered epidemics of smallpox and, probably, measles and influenza. At one point, the natives were virtually eliminated from the coasts of Mexico, and the interior lost nearly 80 per cent of its population. In Peru, almost 90 per cent of the people in the area around present-day Lima died of foreign diseases in less than 50 years.

THE ROCKET IS A MODERN INVENTION

The rocket was invented by the Chinese as far back as 1200 A.D., a century before the cannon. The early rocket consisted of a simple tube into which black gunpowder was poured as a propellant. The first recorded military use of rockets was in the siege of Kaifeng, China in 1232.

The rocket spread to Europe, where its use was recorded in 1258 in Cologne, Germany. Soon, however, the more accurate cannon largely replaced the rocket, which thereafter was used mainly on ships.

In the late 18th century, military interest in rockets was revived and improvements were made in their design, especially by the British.

**THE GUILLOTINE WAS NAMED
AFTER ITS INVENTOR**

The guillotine, a device for chopping off people's heads, was not invented by Dr. Joseph I. Guillotin (1738–1814), although it bears his name.

Dr. Guillotin, a French physician, merely recommended that such a device be developed to kill criminals as swiftly and as painlessly as possible.

It was Dr. Antoine Louis who actually designed the guillotine. After the machine was tested using sheep and dead humans, France officially adopted the guillotine in 1792. It was at first known as the *louisette* after its inventor, but the name of the man who inspired its construction eventually prevailed, much to the chagrin of Dr. Guillotin.

THE BATTLE OF WATERLOO WAS FOUGHT IN WATERLOO

One of the most decisive battles in history, the Battle of Waterloo, was fought on June 18, 1815, by Napoleon Bonaparte against other European armies. Napoleon received his final defeat in the battle. However, in spite of its name, the battle was not fought in Waterloo itself but in a village in Belgium 2 miles (3.2 km) to the south.

FLYING VEHICLES WERE NOT
USED FOR MILITARY PURPOSES
UNTIL WORLD WAR I

Since the first airplane was not flown until the early 1900s, it is commonly supposed that the use of airborne craft for military purposes did not begin until World War I (1914–1918). Actually, the first military air unit was formed in France in 1793, more than a century before World War I.

During the French revolutionary wars, the French government formed a scientific committee for the purpose of getting the best scientists of the day to contribute their knowledge to the war effort. Guyton de Morveau, a balloon enthusiast, suggested that the balloon be put to military use. The balloon, he argued, could be employed to direct armies in the field and to spy on enemy movements. Thus, the first airborne military vehicle was employed.

Military aviation in the United States began in the early years of the Civil War, when balloons were used by the Union forces for reconnaissance. When the war ended, this activity was discontinued, and the military use of aircraft was not revived until World War I, when heavier-than-air craft became commonplace. During World War II, military aviation was accepted for the first time as the equal of the other military services.

CHARLES LINDBERGH FLEW
THE FIRST TRANSATLANTIC FLIGHT

The first person to fly non-stop across the Atlantic was not Charles A. Lindbergh. As a matter of fact, Lindbergh was the sixty-seventh person to make a non-stop flight across that ocean.

In June 1919, long before Lindbergh's flight in 1927, John William Alcock and Arthur Whitten Brown flew from St. Johns, Newfoundland to Ireland in a two-engine Vickers airplane. Thirty-one persons flew non-stop across the Atlantic in the British dirigible R-34 in July 1919. (The R-34, in fact, flew back, making a round-trip crossing.) In October 1924, 33 men crossed the Atlantic aboard the German dirigible LX-216.

Lindbergh was merely the first to make a solo non-stop transatlantic flight.

CHINESE CHECKERS IS CHINESE

The game known as Chinese checkers is a popular game played by two to six players with colored marbles on a hexagonal checkered board. It is a modern version of the 19th-century English game called *Halma* (a Greek word meaning "leap"). The game became popular in the United States in the 1930s. Chinese checkers has nothing at all to do with China.

Chapter 3
Science

ASTRONOMY

COPERNICUS WAS THE FIRST TO ASSERT THAT THE SUN IS THE CENTER OF THE SOLAR SYSTEM

Nicolaus Copernicus (1473–1543), the great Polish scientist who founded modern astronomy, is commonly thought to have been the first to argue that the sun is the center of our planetary system and that the planets, including the earth, revolve around the sun. Actually, it was Aristarchus of Samos who, in the 3rd century B.C., first developed a theory in which the sun, not the earth, held the central position in the solar system.

However, Aristarchus's analysis of the universe was not accepted by his fellow Greeks. After all, didn't their eyes show them what happened in the heavens? The sun rose in the east and set in the west, and the moon and stars turned in the sky. Everything seemed to move but the earth. Therefore, mankind continued to consider the earth to be the center of the universe, the planet around which everything in the heavens revolved. Not until Copernicus was this notion, despite initial resistance, finally abandoned.

UNTIL COLUMBUS PROVED OTHERWISE, PEOPLE THOUGHT THE WORLD WAS FLAT

Not true. As early as the 6th century B.C., Pythagoras of Greece was convinced that the earth was round. The astronomer Claudius Ptolemy in the 2nd century A.D. noted that during an eclipse, the shadow the earth cast on the moon was round. He concluded that it was round because the earth itself was round. Ptolemy also observed that the mast of a ship approaching land is visible before the hull is, and maintained that this could happen only because the earth was spherical.

THE SUN IS FARTHEST
FROM THE EARTH IN WINTER

It is a common but mistaken belief that it is cold in winter because then the sun is farthest from the earth. As a matter of fact, during winter the sun is closer to the earth than during any other season; it is about 3,000,000 miles (4,830,000 km) nearer the earth in the middle of winter than it is in the middle of summer.

The tilt of the earth's axis, not the varying distance of the sun from the earth, determines the change of seasons. When this tilt (slightly more than 23°) is towards the sun, as occurs in summer, the rays of the sun strike the earth more directly (and thus bring more warmth) than when the earth is inclined away from the sun, as happens in winter. (This is so only in the Northern Hemisphere; in the Southern Hemisphere the reverse is true.)

There would be no seasons as we know them if the earth's axis were vertical and not tilted. Constant summer would exist in regions near the equator, and it would always be winter in areas near the poles.

THE SUN REMAINS STATIONARY AS THE EARTH REVOLVES AROUND IT

Every child in elementary school knows that the earth travels around the sun. The earth circles the sun at a rate of 66,500 miles (107,000 km) per hour, and makes a complete orbit every year. What many people do not know is that the sun does not stand still but is also speeding through space.

The entire solar system is revolving around the hub of our local galaxy, the Milky Way, at a tremendous rate of speed. The Milky Way, in turn, is moving even faster around the core of a cluster of galaxies. Finally, the cluster of galaxies is also moving at great speed away from other galaxy clusters.

Does anything in our universe stand still? Scientists say no, nothing.

THE SUN IS A SOLID MASS

It is commonly supposed that the sun consists of solid material similar to that of the earth, the basic difference between the two being that the matter of the sun is at such a high temperature that it burns and gives off light.

Actually, the sun is about 81 per cent hydrogen and 18 per cent helium, containing only about 1 per cent of heavier elements. Since both hydrogen and helium are gases, the sun is really a ball of gas rather than a solid sphere. Nevertheless, the sun is so vast that it constitutes 99.9 per cent of the mass of the entire solar system!

THE MOON SHINES

When people say the moon shines, they are not speaking correctly. The moon, having no light of its own, does not shine; it reflects the light of the sun.

SHOOTING STARS ARE STARS

Shooting or falling stars are not stars but meteors. These masses of matter are material left behind by other bodies in the solar system, and if they enter the earth's gravitational field they fall towards the earth at tremendous speeds of 600 to 2,400 miles (966 km to 3,864 km) per hour. The enormous amount of friction that develops as a meteor plummets through the earth's atmosphere causes it to glow white with heat. When this happens it can be seen from the earth as a shooting or falling star.

A meteor fragment that reaches the ground is called a meteorite. Since all but the largest meteors burn up before they reach the earth, the vast majority of meteorites are no larger than a particle of dust. A few are quite big, however. The largest known meteorite, found in South-West Africa in 1920, weighed 132,000 pounds (59,800 kg).

Scientists estimate that hundreds of millions of meteors (both those that are visible and those that are invisible to the human eye) enter the earth's atmosphere every 24 hours. Although all but a very small number of these are mere specks by the time they reach the earth and no one has yet been killed by a falling meteorite, there is some danger to human life. In September 1954, a woman reported being injured by a meteorite in Sylacauga, Alabama. There is also a report of a Japanese girl being hit a glancing blow by a meteorite. The Field Museum of Natural History in Chicago has an unusual exhibit: a garage roof and an automobile which in 1938 were struck and penetrated by a 3.5-pound (1.6-kg) meteorite in Illinois.

THE PLANETS ARE VISIBLE ONLY AT NIGHT

If you know where to look in the sky, you will be able to see Venus with the naked eye in the daytime for several weeks each year. Incidentally, once in about eight years Venus at night is about twelve times as bright as Sirus, the brightest star in the skies of the Northern Hemisphere.

COMETS AND METEORS ARE THE SAME

Although the two are often thought to be the same, comets and meteors are quite different. A meteor, as we have seen, is a solid piece of material floating in space which, if caught in the earth's gravitational pull, enters the atmosphere at tremendous speed and heats up to white-hot temperatures. Those we see appear to us as fast-moving streaks of light across the sky.

Comets, on the other hand, are frozen chunks of matter—primarily dust, small pieces of rock and solidified gases—that develop "tails" when they approach the sun. Unlike meteors, comets do not become extremely hot; they glow because their tiny particles of matter reflect the light of the sun. Another difference is that, when a comet passes near the sun, it expands to enormous size, becoming many times the size of the earth as the sun's radiation vaporizes its frozen gases and the small solid particles of its head become widely separated. Although both comets and meteors orbit the sun, comets have huge, oval-shaped, stable orbits while those of meteors are smaller and tend to change.

Moreover, although their speed is great, comets, unlike meteors, appear to be motionless spots of light in the sky because they are so far away. Finally, comets may come relatively close to earth but have never entered the planet's atmosphere and struck its surface, while meteors sometimes do. The closest approach was that of Lexell's Comet, which in 1770 came to within 1,500,000 miles (2,413,500 km) of the earth.

ALL MONTHS HAVE A FULL MOON

Not so. The average time from one full moon to another is $29\frac{1}{2}$ days. Since the month of February is shorter than a complete lunar cycle, it can have fewer than four moon phases. The absent phase can be any one of the phases, including the full moon. February has only three phases about every 6 years.

WEATHER

POLAR BEARS PREFER COLD WEATHER

People visiting zoos are in the habit of saying on cold days that it is fine weather for polar bears, while on hot days they feel sorry for these creatures from the far north. It would seem that they are wrong in both instances.

Polar bears soon become acclimated to warmer latitudes and do not appear to suffer in hot weather. Not only do polar bears thrive in the zoos of Europe and America, but they are among the most contented of all animals in captivity. A number of polar bears have reached ripe old ages in the National Zoological Park in Washington, D.C., a city noted for its long, hot summers.

During the extended dark and cold winters in the Arctic, the polar bear develops a thick coat of fur and a heavy layer of fat for protection against the bitter weather. Both the fat and the fur diminish as the warm weather approaches. Polar bears in our zoos, as a rule, do not develop thick coats or heavy layers of fat. They do not like the cold weather as a result. They seldom enter cold water between October and February and seem to welcome the return of spring and summer. One of the polar bear's preferred pastimes is to stretch out with all four feet extended and bask in a blazing sun that would be unbearable for most animals of the temperate zone.

A polar bear born and reared in a warm climate is apt to suffer more from cold than from heat.

THE OCEAN NEVER FREEZES

It is commonly thought that the oceans do not freeze over. This is not true. If it gets cold enough, ocean water, in fact, will freeze. Unlike fresh water, however, ocean water has no fixed freezing point. The temperature at which ice begins to form in the sea depends on the salt content of the water. At a salt content of 35 parts per thousand, the approximate average for the oceans, the freezing point is 28.6°F (–1.89°C).

Sea ice is not to be confused with icebergs, however. Icebergs are huge chunks of ice broken off from glaciers in the Northern Hemisphere or broken off from the Antarctic ice shelf in the Southern Hemisphere. Icebergs are therefore land ice made from fresh water in contrast to sea ice which is formed by the freezing of sea water at the ocean's surface. The thickness of sea ice seldom exceeds 10 feet (3m), while icebergs may be hundreds of feet thick.

Not only are there large ice fields in the colder regions towards the poles, but snow drifts as well. Snow falling on water near the freezing point or above does not sink. It floats on the surface. Beds of several feet thick can pile up in snow banks as a result.

A RAINDROP IS ROUND OR PEAR-SHAPED

The popular image of a raindrop is that it is shaped somewhat like a pear with a rounded bottom tapering to a point on top, or that it is perfectly round. Neither is correct.

High-speed photography of raindrops nearing the earth show them to be shaped like mushroom caps. The bottoms of the raindrops are flat and the tops are rounded. The shape is a result of air resistance. As the raindrop falls, the air resistance exerts a force on the raindrop, flattening it. The flattening on the bottom causes the top to bulge outwards.

MOST LIGHTNING VICTIMS ARE INSTANTLY KILLED

On the contrary, most people struck by lightning recover completely, and many more would survive if bystanders came to their assistance instead of assuming them to be dead.

People hit by lightning often stop breathing, and artificial respiration should be given as soon as possible. Once the victim's breathing resumes, he may be examined and treated for burns.

Sometimes the heart stops, but the victim can often be revived by external massage.

Another reason many lightning victims do not receive immediate assistance by bystanders is the completely mistaken notion that a person struck by lightning retains electricity and can give a shock. The victim's body is perfectly safe to touch.

COLD WEATHER IS DEADLY TO ORANGE TREES

It is widely assumed that cold is destructive to orange trees. One often reads in the newspapers about widespread damage to orange crops caused by freezing weather.

Actually, oranges thrive best where trees are chilled somewhat by occasional light frosts in winter. The orange tree is dormant or semi-dormant in winter, and temperatures at freezing or a few degrees below freezing not only do no damage to orange trees during winter, but are good for the trees.

The problem with cold weather develops when either the temperature drops too far below freezing, or occurs outside of winter when the orange tree is not dormant or semi-dormant but instead is growing or flowering. In either case, smudge pots or other heating devices must be used to prevent damage. Moderate freezing at the right season is actually welcomed by orange growers. Orange trees do not thrive in continual heat.

This is also borne out by the fact that oranges grown in frost-free tropical climates are inferior in appearance and taste to those grown in colder, more temperature climates. Cool temperatures at night seem to be important in the development of a brilliant orange hue and in the quality of taste. Orange trees are not addicted to heat, as is commonly supposed, but require a certain amount of cold.

SNOW IS FROZEN RAIN

Snow is commonly thought to be frozen rain. Snowflakes are actually formed directly from water vapor without going through any liquid or rain state.

Snow originates when water vapor condenses on a tiny, microscopic particle floating in the air.

When the water vapor condenses on this small particle, called a nucleus, in temperatures at or below freezing, a minute ice crystal is formed. The resulting snow crystal is about one hundredth of an inch (.025 cm) in diameter. As these tiny ice crystals are suspended in moist air, further condensation of water vapor increases the size of the ice crystal.

In cold weather or in colder regions, these snow crystals fall to earth as they are. In warmer regions, falling snow crystals tend to stick together to form still larger units called snowflakes. Snowflakes larger than one inch (2.54 cm) in diameter are not unknown.

If the temperature near the earth is above freezing, the snowflakes often melt before they reach the surface of the earth and come down as rain. It is estimated that as much as half of all rain falling to earth is due to the melting of snowflakes as they approach earth. Modern rainmaking techniques, in fact, involve producing snow crystals in the upper air. This is accomplished by scattering dry ice in the atmosphere. The resulting snow crystals and snowflakes melt as they near the surface of the earth and become rain.

LONDON IS A WET PLACE

London must be a wet place. How else can one explain why Englishmen are seldom without raincoats or umbrellas. While it is true that the weather is generally cloudy and some rain is likely to fall on half the days of the year, London is not a particularly wet place measured by total annual precipitation.

London has an annual precipitation of 23.4 inches (595 mm). New York, by comparison, has an average annual precipitation of 42.37 inches (1,076 mm), while around the world the average annual rainfall is about 40 inches (1,016 mm). In terms of annual precipitation, London is a rather dry place.

ICELAND IS A VERY COLD COUNTRY

Many people suppose that Iceland is a cold country because of its name and its location just south of the Arctic Circle. But Iceland is not a frozen, unpleasant land. The average January temperature in Reykjavik, the capital of Iceland, is about 30°F (–1.1°C). Thus, winters are not much colder in Reykjavik than in New York City or the cities of Western Europe, while summers are cooler and more comfortable.

How can a land so far north have such a moderate climate? Warm ocean currents called the Gulf Stream help to prevent extremely cold weather, and the many hot springs throughout Iceland keep the ground rather warm, even in winter.

THE EARTH:
LAND AND SEA

THE EARTH'S CRUST IS A SOLID

The single most plentiful element making up the earth's crust turns out not to be a solid, but a gas. Oxygen makes up nearly 47 per cent of the solid, rocky portion of the earth's crust. It also constitutes about 89 per cent by weight of all the water in the world. Adding the oxygen content of the land to that of the water portions of the earth, oxygen compounds make up about 50 per cent of the earth's crust. These compounds, of course, are solids and liquids. But oxygen in the free state is a gas.

THE SKY IS BLUE

The sky is not blue; it has no color of its own. The blue color of the sky is the result of what happens to sunlight as it travels through the atmosphere.

Sunlight is a combination of all the colors in the rainbow. As it passes through the atmosphere, millions of small particles suspended in the air scatter the sunlight. Blue light, since it has a short wavelength, is more readily scattered than reds and yellows, which have longer wavelengths. The sky is lit up, so to speak, by the blue light contained in sunlight.

The ocean is blue for the same reason. The blue of the sea is caused by the scattering of sunlight by tiny suspended particles in the water. The emptier the water, the bluer it appears. The presence of microscopic plant life makes the water green, brown or even reddish.

THE CANARY ISLANDS ARE NAMED AFTER THE BIRD

All varieties of domestic canaries are descendants of the wild canary. The wild canary is a native of Madeira, the Azores and the Canary Islands. Although the canary bird is in fact named after the Canary Islands, the islands themselves owe their name to another animal.

The Romans called the islands *Insulae Canariae*, which means "islands of the dogs." The Romans gave the islands the name because so many canines, or dogs, lived there. The Canary Islands, therefore, are not named after birds but after dogs.

NORTH AMERICA IS DIRECTLY
NORTH OF SOUTH AMERICA

A glimpse at any map will quickly dispel any notion that North and South American lie directly north and south of each other. All of Alaska, 85 per cent of Canada, 90 per cent of the contiguous 48 States, all of Mexico, and all of Central America with the exception of Panama, lie to the west of South America.

North and South America are misnamed. East and West America would have been more accurate.

AFRICA IS SOUTH OF EUROPE

The four southernmost provinces of Spain are actually farther south than are some parts of North Africa. The Spanish provinces that lie farther south than the northernmost part of Africa are Cádiz, Málaga, Granada and Almería.

THE GEOGRAPHIC AND
MAGNETIC POLES ARE THE SAME

The magnetic poles are, in fact, at a considerable distance from the geographic poles. They are about 11.5° away from the geographic poles, the equivalent of several hundred miles. In addition the magnetic poles are not fixed but have a tendency to wander about a bit from year to year, and to wander about considerably over longer periods of time.

Geological evidence indicates that the magnetic poles have been located in almost every part of the globe at some point in history. It is also known that the magnetic poles reverse themselves completely over thousands of years. When this takes place, the magnetic north becomes south, and vice versa. Scientists have counted 171 magnetic reversals in the last 76,000,000 years.

The geographic and magnetic poles are far from being the same.

THE PANAMA CANAL RUNS EAST-WEST

The Panama Canal does not run east-west. Any detailed map of the area would show that the direction is actually northeast-southwest.

If you look at the map again, you will see that the Panama Canal runs from the northeast to the southwest, but the entire country of Panama runs east-west. Because the Isthmus of Panama curves in a snakelike fashion, however, Panama is the only place on earth where one can go east to the Pacific Ocean and west to the Atlantic Ocean. An arm of the Pacific Ocean extends east of a part of the Caribbean coast, which is part of the Atlantic Ocean. This means, also, that in a large area of Panama the sun rises in the Pacific and sets in the Atlantic.

A STRAIGHT LINE IS THE SHORTEST DISTANCE BETWEEN TWO POINTS

A straight line may be the shortest distance between two points in geometry, but not necessarily in human travels. The shortest distance between New York and London, for example, is along the great circle route which follows the curvature of the earth. Seen from directly overhead, the line of the great circle route certainly looks straight enough. Viewed from the side, however, it is curved as it follows the shape of the earth.

In theory, a straight line could be drawn between London and New York assuming one could travel through and under the earth. As a practical matter, however, the shortest distance between widely separated points on earth is actually a curve.

VOLCANOES ARE ERUPTIONS OF MOLTEN MATERIAL FROM THE EARTH'S INTERIOR

The earth is commonly pictured as having a thin but solid skin resting on a molten interior. Volcanoes are viewed as eruptions of molten material bursting through the thin skin of the earth's surface. This is how volcanoes were, in fact, explained historically.

Geologists now know from the study of earthquakes that the earth is solid down to a depth of 1,800 miles (2,880 km). Below that level, the earth is believed to be molten. However, there is no possibility that the molten material is able to travel through the solid 1,800-mile (2,880-km) barrier to reach the surface.

These, as well as other observations, have led geologists to the conclusion that the reservoirs of molten material from which volcanoes erupt are small in area and are located near the surface. The small pockets of molten material come from depths of no more than 20 miles (32 km) on the average.

Nor is the fact that volcanoes erupt from near the surface a recent phenomenon. Throughout the stretch of known geological time (about 3,000,000,000 years) the earth has remained structurally the same. Volcanoes have always, within geological time, come from pools of molten material close to the surface of the earth, rather than from deeper in the earth or from the earth's interior.

DESERTS ARE MOSTLY SAND

One thinks of the desert as a vast, uniform expanse of sand, swept up here and there into dunes. The picture of the desert is not correct.

The largest continuously sandy desert is the Rub al-Khali (Arabic for empty quarter) located in the Arabian peninsula. The Rub al-Khali, however, is only one third of the total area of the Arabian Desert. The other two thirds are barren, sun-scorched rocky plains. Another large desert is the Gobi Desert in the Far East. Except for a few sand dunes in the southwest, the Gobi Desert is largely plateau land covered with small stones smoothed by wind erosion. The largest desert in the world, the Sahara, is but 20 per cent sand. The remainder of the surface of the Sahara is barren rock, rocky plateau, or gravel-covered plain.

Nor are inland sand dunes found only in desert areas. Dunes can be started wherever there is enough loose sand, wind to move it, and an obstacle to stop the sand. Miniature sandy deserts can be found even in the middle of well-watered forested areas.

To the geographer and the geologist, deserts are more rocky than sandy.

MIRAGES OCCUR ONLY IN HOT PLACES

Mirages are popularly associated with conditions of extreme heat. The ever-receding puddle on the sizzling highway surface, the unreachable oasis in the desert, are what come to mind when one thinks of a mirage. Mirages are actually as common under conditions of cold as they are under conditions of heat. Mirages associated with the Arctic are, in fact, larger and more enduring than those associated with the desert.

Arctic mirages differ from their desert counterparts in that they reflect something that actually exists, although not in the place it is located. Thus the traveller in the desert may see a lake

that is not really there. The traveller in the Arctic may see a land that exists but not in the place he sees it.

Whether an image has a real or imaginary origin, all mirages can be photographed. The lens of the camera reacts to any mirage as does the human eye.

EUROPE AND ASIA ARE
TWO DISTINCT CONTINENTS

Europe and Asia are commonly regarded as two distinct continents. They are merely vast geographical divisions of the greater single land mass known as Eurasia. There is not—and never has been—a clear geographical boundary between them. The separation of the two is a matter of drawing an arbitrary line and calling one part Europe and the other Asia, based solely on custom or tradition.

There is no narrowing of the land mass between Asia and Europe that could serve as a clear-cut geographic division marking where one ends and the other begins, as there is between North America and South America (the Isthmus of Panama) or between Africa and Eurasia (the Isthmus of Suez).

DIG A DEEP ENOUGH HOLE
IN THE UNITED STATES
AND IT WILL REACH CHINA

Any two places on opposite sides of the earth, so situated that a straight line from one place to the other passes through the middle of the earth, are called the antipodes (pronounced an-TIP-oh-deez) of each other.

Many people believe that China is the antipodes of the United States. Thus, if a deep enough hole were dug in the United States and passed through the midpoint of the earth, the hole would come up somewhere in China. This is simply not the case. Both China and the United States are, in fact, in the northern hemisphere. The true antipodes of the United States is an area of the Indian Ocean west of Australia and east of South Africa.

The approximate antipodes of London is the Antipodes Islands, a cluster of rocky, uninhabited islands in the South Pacific Ocean 460 miles (750 km) southeast of New Zealand.

SUNLIGHT REACHES ALL PARTS OF THE WORLD

The total surface area of the earth is 197,000,000 square miles (510,000,000 km^2) of which 59,000,000 square miles (153,000,000 km^2) is land. This means that 71 per cent of the earth's surface is water. The average depth of this water being nearly 3 miles (5 km), more than half of the earth's surface is actually covered with water so deep that no sunlight is able to penetrate to the bottom. Thus, more than half of the earth's crust never receives any sunlight at any time, and is in a state of perpetual darkness.

135

IT IS HOT EVERYWHERE ON THE EQUATOR

Not on tall mountains located in this zone. Africa's Mount Kenya lies just south of the equator, is 17,040 feet (5,194 m) high and has several glaciers on its upper regions. Mount Chimborazo near the equator in the Andes of Ecuador is also permanently snow-capped. It is therefore possible to freeze to death at or near the equator.

QUICKSAND DRAGS YOU UNDER

Quicksand does not pull the unwary victim down beneath its surface. Getting stuck in quicksand does not mean automatic death.

Quicksand, a mixture of sand and water, is about twice as buoyant as water, and one can take advantage of this buoyancy to get free. Of course, anyone who stumbles into quicksand, becomes hysterical and beings to thrash about wildly in an effort to escape will only work his body in deeper, and may indeed "sink up to his neck." However, the quicksand would not be pulling; the victim would be doing the pushing.

If caught in quicksand, experts advise, remain calm and free yourself by lying on your back, letting the buoyancy of the quicksand support you, and slowly rolling towards firm ground again.

DURING EARTHQUAKES, PEOPLE ARE SWALLOWED UP BY THE EARTH

During an earthquake it is very unlikely that the ground will open up, cause people to fall in and then close on its unlucky victims. Throughout recorded history, only in one instance has this happened. In 1948, during an earthquake in Fukui, Japan, a woman fell into a newly opened crack in the earth, which quickly closed in on her up to the height of her chin. She died instantly. A cow was also killed in this way during the San Francisco earthquake of 1906.

Most casualties during and immediately after earthquakes are caused by the collapse of buildings. In the great Shensi earthquake of 1556, some 830,000 Chinese died when the homes in which they lived caved in.

EARTHQUAKES IN THE UNITED STATES ARE CONFINED TO THE WEST

New England actually has the second highest number of earthquakes after California. While the earthquakes are small and have not killed anyone since the 1600s, when the Pilgrims began to keep records, New England averages four to six earthquakes a month. The region's worst earthquake occurred in 1775. This quake destroyed much of Portsmouth, N.H. and toppled the weathervane on top of Boston's famous Faneuil Hall. Geologists have been unable to explain why New England should be so prone to earthquake activity since the region does not lie along fault lines nor is it close to major geological plates.

MOUNT EVEREST IS THE HIGHEST MOUNTAIN IN THE WORLD

Yes and no. It all depends on how you measure height. Mount Everest in the Himalaya Mountains, rising 29,028 feet (8,848 m) above sea level, is considered the tallest mountain in the world. No other mountain rises so high above sea level. However, measuring height according to distance above sea level is only one way of doing it.

Another equally valid way is to measure height on the basis of distance from the center of the earth. If this method is used, Ecuador's Mount Chimborazo in the Andes Mountains, which rises "only" 20,577 feet (6,272 m) above sea level, is taller.

Mount Chimborazo happens to be about two degrees from the equator, while Mount Everest is far north of the equator. Since the earth is not perfectly round but bulges at the equator, Chimborazo by this measurement is nearly 2 miles (3.2 km) higher than Mount Everest.

THE HIMALAYA MOUNTAINS ARE THE GREATEST IN THE WORLD

The greatest mountain range in the world is not even visible, for the most part. Undiscovered until this century, it lies under the Atlantic Ocean between the North American and European continents, and is called the Mid-Atlantic Ridge.

This gigantic underwater formation extends in a north-south direction from Iceland to near the Antarctic Circle, a distance of more than 10,000 miles (16,090 km). The Himalaya range, in comparison, is a mere 1,600 miles (2,574 km) long.

Because the water in this part of the Atlantic is so deep, most of these huge mountains lie far below the surface. The peaks of some of the larger mountains rise above the ocean, however, forming such islands as the Azores, Ascension, St. Paul and St. Helena.

THE POLAR REGIONS ARE VERY SIMILAR

Most people have only a vague idea of what the polar regions are like, and think the Arctic (northernmost) and the Antarctic (southernmost) regions are pretty much the same. However, there are a number of differences between the two.

The average temperature of the Antarctic at a given latitude is about 20°F (11°C) colder than the temperature at the same latitude in the Arctic. The Antarctic is by far the coldest region in the world, one reason being that it is a mountainous land mass. The Antarctic averages 14,000 feet (4,267 m) above sea level. The Arctic, by comparison, is for the most part at or near sea level.

As for summers, the temperature in the Antarctic seldom gets above freezing. The summers in the Arctic are brief but can get as hot as New York does.

Almost 95 per cent of the world's permanent ice is found in the Antarctic. The covering of ice and snow on the Antarctic land mass has an average thickness of 8,000 feet (2,438 m). The thickness of the ice pack around the North Pole, on the other hand, averages 9 to 10 feet (2.7 to 3 m) thick, although in some areas the ice may be as thick as 65 feet (19.8 m).

Life is far more abundant in the Arctic than in the Antarctic. In the Arctic are vast herds of caribou and reindeer, as well as the polar bear, seal, walrus, and many kinds of birds and insects. While plant life is not as varied as in more southerly regions, the Arctic does have 1,500 different kinds of plants. The Antarctic, by comparison, has little more than penguins, seals, whales, a few insect species, and some lichens and mosses.

Of course, the final proof that the Arctic is a more livable place than the Antarctic is the presence of human life there—Eskimos, Lapps and other peoples. Except for visiting explorers and scientists, no humans live or have ever lived in the Antarctic.

SEA LIFE IS MOST ABUNDANT IN WARM WATER

It seems perfectly reasonable to suppose that marine life is more abundant in warm water than it is in cold water. After all, life on land is more plentiful in warm than it is in cold climates, ought not the same to apply to marine life? The answer, surprisingly, turns out to be the reverse. Marine life of all kinds, both animal and vegetable, is more abundant in cold waters than it is in warm.

Cold water supports more marine life because it is able to hold more dissolved gases, particularly oxygen and carbon dioxide. The oxygen is vital to animal life, while the carbon dioxide is necessary to marine plants for photosynthesis.

Antarctic waters, especially the current known as the Antarctic Convergence, give an example of a body of cold water teeming with marine plant and animal life. The Antarctic Convergence is so thick with plant plankton and small animals such as the shrimp-like krill, that it is referred to as a "soup." The soup supports a great chain including fish, whales, sharks and seals. The waters of the Antarctic Convergence have the richest marine life in the world.

ALL LIFE IS SUBJECT TO DEATH FROM OLD AGE

Bacteria and other single-celled organisms do not die from old age. So long as their growth requirements are met, bacteria will continue to grow and multiply by dividing without end. Death from age is inevitable only among the higher multi-cellular organisms. Single-celled organisms remain perpetually young. Bacteria and other single-celled organisms can be killed in many ways, to be sure, but they do not die from aging as do the higher life forms.

AS YOU LISTEN TO A SHELL, YOU CAN HEAR THE ROAR OF THE SEA

When you hold a seashell close to your ear, the noise you hear is a combination of ordinary sounds coming from outside the shell in your immediate surroundings. Because of the peculiar shape of the shell and the smoothness of its interior, the sound from outside the shell is echoed and rc-cchocd as thc air inside the hollow shell vibrates. These echoes blend together to produce the roaring sound you hear. Among the sounds picked up and amplified is the sound of blood rushing through your ear.

BACTERIA ARE HARMFUL

Bacteria are thought to be bad because they cause disease. However, not all bacteria are bad.

Most bacteria are not only harmless but many are useful, if not essential. Without certain bacteria in the digestive tract, for example, food could not be digested. Bacteria are also vital links in the recycling of formerly living things. Bacteria break down dead organic matter so it can be reused by living things.

Bacteria are also economically important. Nitrogen-fixing bacteria convert nitrogen from the air into a form that can be utilized by legumes such as peas, alfalfa, peanuts and clover. While some bacteria may be responsible for food spoilage, other bacteria are essential in the making of yogurt, buttermilk, cheese, vinegar, sauerkraut and other foods. Bacterial action is especially important these days because it is used in making certain kinds of alcohol to power automobiles.

Bacteria are not all bad, we must conclude, just as snakes are not all poisonous.

BACTERIA DO NOT REPRODUCE SEXUALLY

Although bacteria generally reproduce by simple cell division, certain bacteria do in fact mate on occasion by a method resembling sexual reproduction. The process is known as conjugation. Two bacteria touch and then, through a hole that appears in the cell walls, there is a transfer of genetic material from one to the other. The bacteria consist of a donor, referred to as a male, and a recipient, referred to as a female. This is one way in which genetic material is exchanged in bacteria.

Researchers have found that the female bacteria of the species *Streptococcus faecalis*, a normal inhabitant of the human intestine, can signal to potential mates that they are ready to conjugate. The female secretes a substance which attracts nearby males and causes them to clump around her.

PLANTS

BANANAS GROW ON TREES

If by a tree one means a plant with a woody trunk that survives from one season to the next, then there is no such thing as a banana tree. The banana fruit actually grows on a stalk. While the

banana plant may reach a height of 30 feet (9.1 m), and resembles a tree in size and shape, it does not have a woody trunk. The stalk consists of the lower ends of the leaves, which overlap and are tightly bound together.

The banana plant bears fruit for only a single season. Then the portion above ground dies, leaving an underground stem which grows into a new banana plant the following season.

THE PEANUT IS A NUT

The peanut is not a nut. Most nuts grow on trees. The peanut plant is a legume, a member of the pea family, the peanuts it produces grow underground.

TREES RECEIVE MOST OF THEIR NUTRITION THROUGH THEIR ROOTS

Not so. Roots are necessary to the tree because they anchor it, and because they take up moisture and minerals from the soil. However, the leaves play an even more important role in the nutrition of the tree. Leaves, using chlorophyll (the substance which makes them green), are able to convert carbon dioxide and water into food in the presence of sunlight. This process is called photosynthesis. Is in the leaves, not in the roots, that the manufacture of food for the entire tree goes on.

EVERY TREE HAS ONLY ONE KIND OF LEAF

Not the sassafras tree. This tree, a common North American member of the laurel family, has leaves of three distinctly different shapes. One kind of leaf is basically oval and unlobed, another is shaped like a mitten with a thumb on one side, and the third is three-lobed with "thumbs" on both sides. All three of these leaves may be found on the same tree, and even on the same twig at the same time.

The leaves of mulberry trees also have various shapes.

A TREE GROWS BY LENGTHENING
ITS ENTIRE TRUNK

Most people, if asked, would assume that a tree grows pretty much like other living things—that the trunk merely stretches upwards as the tree grows. This is not really what happens.

Actually, a tree grows in height as a result of cell division and enlargement that occurs only at the top of the trunk. Thus, a tree gains height through the growth of new wood at its uppermost region. A tree gains thickness because cells in the outer layer of the trunk also divide and increase in number, adding new layers. So, a tree can be said to grow as a result of the gradual accumulation of wood, layer upon layer, extending up the outside of the trunk and over the top. This growth pattern is the reason why the branches of a tree do not rise higher above the ground as the tree grows taller, and explains why two nails driven into a tree trunk close together do not drift apart over the years as the tree increases in circumference.

The branches and twigs of the tree grow in the same way.

REDWOODS ARE THE OLDEST TREES

The huge redwood trees of California (also called sequoias) grow to be very old—several thousand years old, in fact—but they are not the oldest trees. "General Sherman," the name given to a giant sequoia in Sequoia National Park in California, is the largest living thing in the world:

272 feet (83 m) high and 37 feet (11 m) in diameter at the thickest part of its trunk. However, it has been around a mere 3,500 years.

A far less spectacular tree in height and width, the bristlecone pine, often reaches this age and even exceeds it. This tree is usually found at elevations above 10,000 feet (3,048 m) in the American West, and a specimen 4,000 years old is not uncommon. The oldest known specimen, 4,600 years old and aptly named "Methuselah," was found in the White Mountains in California. The potential life span of a bristlecone pine is estimated to be 6,000 years. The giant redwoods are babies by comparison.

FOREST FIRES ARE HARMFUL TO ALL TREES

Some trees, surprisingly, need forest fires to survive. The cones of the jack pine open and release seeds only after exposure to intense heat. In this way nature insures that the jack pine will grow again after a forest fire.

THE CENTURY PLANT BLOSSOMS
EVERY HUNDRED YEARS

The century plant got its name under false pretenses, because of the mistaken notion that it blossoms only when it reaches 100 years. The fact is that no century plant even survives such a period of time.

How long it takes the plant to blossom depends on the plant and on the conditions under which it is growing. In warmer climates, the plants may blossom every 5 to 10 years. In cooler climates, especially the United States, the plants generally take longer to blossom, sometimes as much as 20 or 30 years. The plant may grow 60 years or so, at most, before it blossoms.

RICE PAPER IS MADE FROM RICE

Rice paper is not derived from rice. It is made from the pith, or inner part of the trunk, of a small tree, *Aralia (Fatsia) papyrifera*. The tree grows in many portions of Taiwan and is 10 to 15 feet (3 to 4.6 m) in height. The Japanese call the tree *tsuso*, the Chinese, *tung tsao*.

ORCHIDS ARE RARE FLOWERS

Orchids may be expensive, but they are far from rare. On the contrary, the orchid family is regarded by botanists as the largest family of plants in the world. Since new orchids are continually being discovered, it is difficult to arrive at an accurate estimate of the number of orchids. Educated guesses range from 15,000 to 35,000 species in 400 to 800 genera. In addition to natural orchids, there are thousands of man-made hybrids.

Nor are orchids found in limited areas, as is commonly thought. While most orchids are found in tropical and subtropical regions, orchids grow over much of the globe, from the Arctic Circle to the tropics, from sea level to over 10,000 feet (3,048 m). About the only place orchids are rarely found is in the desert.

POISON IVY IS IVY; POISON OAK IS OAK

Poison ivy is a North American climbing plant, *Rhus radicans*. It causes an irritating and painful rash on the skin of many people. In spite of its name, however, poison ivy is not a member of the ivy family, but belongs in the cashew family.

Poison oak, another plant closely related to poison ivy and producing similar unpleasant results in many people, is not an oak. It is also a member of the cashew family.

THE MOISTURE SEEN ON PLANTS IN THE MORNING IS DEW

The moisture on leaves and grass observed in the morning on plants may not necessarily be dew. This moisture often comes from the plant itself.

Plants exude moisture in a little-known process called guttation. Guttation usually occurs in young leaves during cool, humid nights following hot days. Droplets of moisture remain on the leaves until morning. When they are seen, they are easily mistaken for dew.

METALS, MINERALS AND GEMS

PEARLS ARE FOUND IN EDIBLE OYSTERS

At optimist has been defined as a man who goes into a restaurant without money and orders a meal of oysters, intending to pay for his meal with the pearl he expects to find. The poor soul will no doubt end up paying for his dinner by washing dishes!

Although it is possible to find a pearl occasionally in an edible North American oyster, these have no value as gems. Pearls of gem quality are found only in a rather small percentage of oysters that live in tropical waters, especially in the Persian Gulf area.

LEAD IS THE HEAVIEST METAL

Definitely not. Twelve other metals are heavier. They are: gold, iridium, mercury, osmium, palladium, platinum, rhodium, ruthenium, tantalum, thalium, tungsten, uranium.

LEAD PENCILS CONTAIN LEAD

The modern lead pencil contains no lead at all. The writing part of the pencil is made of graphite, a soft, crystallized form of carbon, mixed with clay for hardness. The more clay, the harder the pencil.

Graphite has often been confused with lead—hence the name "lead pencil"—but it is a separate, unrelated substance.

TIN CANS ARE MADE OF TIN

The tin can is really a steel can with a tiny amount of tin added. Tin is far too expensive to be used to make tin cans, which are used once and thrown away. Instead, tin cans are made from sheets of rolled steel to which a very thin coat of tin has been applied.

ALL GEMS ARE MINERALS

At least four gems are not minerals: pearl, coral, amber, and jet. Pearls are formed in oysters and other shellfish when these mollusks secrete a substance that hardens in layer upon layer around an irritating object (such as a grain of sand) that has become embedded in their soft tissues. Coral is the hard skeletons of small ocean creatures called polyps. Amber is the hardened remains of sap from prehistoric pine trees and other evergreens. Jet is a black form of lignite, a substance that resembles coal.

THE DIAMOND IS THE MOST VALUABLE GEM

This isn't true. Carat for carat, the ruby is more valuable than the diamond.

THE DIAMOND IS VALUABLE
BECAUSE IT IS SO RARE

The diamond is not a rare gem—uncommon, yes, but not rare. It is mined in many African countries, several other parts of the world, and also under the sea. The diamond, in fact, is the most common of all the gems, but is nevertheless an expensive, prized mineral for two reasons. First of all, it is beautiful. Second, it is costly to cut and polish because if its hardness.

THE DIAMOND IS THE TOUGHEST GEM

Diamond is the hardest natural substance known but it is not particularly tough. The toughest gem known is jade, whose tightly interlaced fibers keep it intact despite repeated blows with a hammer. A diamond, on the other hand, is a single crystal which, if hit at the right point, will shatter.

Because of jade's interlocking structure, it can be carved into delicate shapes without risking fracture.

"DIAMONDS ARE FOREVER"

Although diamonds are the hardest of all known substances, they are not indestructible. Diamonds were once thought to be unbreakable. They were sometimes tested with hammer blows, often with sad results. Diamonds, as we now know, can be shattered with a single sharp blow at the right spot.

Diamonds will also burn. Depending on the hardness of the diamond, a diamond will begin to burn at a temperature of 1400°F to 1600°F (760°C to 875°C). Thousands of diamonds were burned up in the great San Francisco fire of 1906. It is estimated that temperatures as high as 2200°F (1200°C) were reached in that fire.

The reason diamonds burn is that they consist of pure carbon, the same element found in coal and oil. Diamond, in fact, has the distinction of being the only gem containing a single element. All other gems are compounds of two or more elements.

Chapter 4
Creatures

MAMMALS

MAMMALS AROSE AFTER DINOSAURS DIED OUT

It is not true, as many people believe, that mammals appeared only after the last of the dinosaurs became extinct about 70,000,000 years ago. Mammals and dinosaurs actually lived together for an enormous stretch of geological time.

Primitive mammals are first detected in the fossils of the Jurassic period about 165,000,000 years ago. It is also during this period that *Stegosaurus, Allosaurus, Brontosaurus,* and other famous dinosaurs arose. Mammals and dinosaurs, therefore, lived together for a period of about 95,000,000 years, a long period by any standard. The early mammals may not have seemed impressive as they scurried about between the legs of the giant dinosaurs, but they were there.

ALL ANIMALS CRAVE SALT

No. All animals lose a certain amount of salt each day, and must replace it to remain healthy. However, some diets provide more salt than others. Animals which feed exclusively on plants (cattle, horses, antelopes, and so on) crave salt because they do not get enough from their normal diet. Carnivorous (meat-eating) and omnivorous (meat- and plant-eating) animals (including man), on the other hand, have no such need to supplement their diets with salt; they get all the salt they need from the blood and flesh of the animals they eat.

ALL ANIMALS LIE DOWN TO SLEEP

Humans only have to lie down to sleep well, but many animals do not. The horse, for one, sleeps far better standing up than lying down. Horses have been known to go for months on end without lying down. However, both horses and cattle, especially when in herds, may lie down, one at a time, with legs outstretched and sleep deeply for several minutes.

The horse can relax and sleep while standing up because its leg joints automatically lock in place to support the animal. It is as if the animal were standing on stilts.

Elephants, zebras, antelopes and many other plant-eating animals are also able to sleep on their feet.

NO ANIMAL CAN SEE BEHIND
ITS BACK WHILE FACING FORWARD

Hunters who have approached rabbits from behind only to have them scurry off know this is not so. Because a rabbit's eyes are set on the side of its head and protrude somewhat, it can virtually see in a full circle (as well as upwards) even when its head remains motionless.

Antelope, deer and other animals that need to be alert to avoid being killed by predators also have this kind of vision.

THE SIZE OF A NEWBORN ANIMAL
DEPENDS ON THE SIZE OF ITS PARENTS

Not necessarily. The size and condition of an animal at birth often depend more on where it is born and the circumstances of its infancy than on the size it will be when it reaches adulthood. The newborn of many species of deer and antelope are large in relation to the size of their parents, and quite strong, able to stand and walk shakily very soon after coming into the world. Why? These animals are in many cases required to move with the herd almost immediately after birth. They must rely on speed to avoid being caught and killed by other animals, which often seek out the young when attacking a herd.

Black bears of North America, on the other hand, are quite small at birth. Adults usually weigh between 200 and 300 pounds (91 and 136 kg), and individuals weighing 600 pounds (272 kg) have been reported. The bear cub, however, is born blind, toothless, hairless and helpless in a den in the middle of winter, weighs only 8 ounces (.23 kg) and is about 8 inches (20.3 cm) long. The bear can afford to begin life so weak and helpless because it is cared for by its mother for at least the first year of its life. Unlike the young deer and antelope, it does not have to face problems immediately after birth.

The newborn of many marsupials (animals having pouches in which the young are carried) are also far smaller than one might expect. A kangaroo is about an inch (2.5 cm) long when born; an opossum at birth is about the size of a bumblebee and weighs $1/15$ of an ounce (1.9 g).

ALL ANIMALS DRINK

No. All animals need water, but not all animals get their water by drinking. The kangaroo rat, an inhabitant of desert regions in the southwestern United States, is able to get along without drinking water, getting its moisture from the plants it eats. Other animals very seldom drink water. Giraffes can go for weeks without drinking. They, too, manage to get enough moisture from the foliage they feed on. Most sheep and gazelles drink infrequently. A few lizards are able to meet their water needs largely by absorbing it through their pores.

ANIMAL LITTERS ARE ALWAYS
A MIXTURE OF MALE AND FEMALE

While it is generally true that animal litters contain members of both sexes, there is at least one exception. The nine-banded armadillo gives birth to four babies of one sex at a time—always either all male or all female. Are the numbers of male and female born equal in all animals? Again, this is generally so, but with an interesting exception. Among greyhound dogs, more males are born than females. For every 100 female greyhounds, 110 males are born.

THE WHALE SPOUTS WATER

When a whale "blows," it looks as if it is spouting water but it is really blowing out air.

Before a whale dives, it fills its huge lungs with air, and it can hold its breath for as long as an hour before it surfaces. When the whale comes up to the surface again, it blows out the air in a great blast through one or two nostrils, called blowholes, on top of its head. When this air, which has become warm and moist in the whale's lungs, meets the colder air of the atmosphere, it condenses into a steamy vapor. The colder the air around the whale, the more visible the vapor when the whale exhales. Much the same thing happens to humans on a cold day, when we can "see our breath" as we exhale.

Thus, the whale does not spout water. A true mammal, it can no more tolerate water in its breathing system than we can.

ELEPHANTS ARE AFRAID OF MICE

This is a common belief that has been around a long time, but there is not the slightest particle of truth to it. Mice often infest the cages of elephants in zoos and circuses, but no keeper has ever reported any elephant even mildly upset by the little animals. Usually, the mice scurrying after food on the floor of the cage are simply ignored by the elephants.

THE ELEPHANT DRINKS WITH ITS TRUNK

The elephant does not take water in through its trunk. It drinks with its mouth just as we do, but first it sucks water into its trunk. It then inserts its trunk into its mouth, lets the water out there, and swallows it.

How do baby elephants nurse? The trunk is pushed aside during suckling and the baby elephant uses its mouth to obtain nourishment, as do all mammals.

THE HIPPOPOTAMUS SWEATS BLOOD

The skin of the hippopotamus does secrete a thick, oily, reddish substance that gathers in droplets on the skin. This secretion helps to prevent the animal's thick hide from drying and cracking, especially when the hippo is out of water. The protective fluid flows more freely and becomes a darker red when the animal is hot, excited or in pain. However, although it resembles blood in color and texture, the fluid is not blood and has no blood in it.

THE BEST WAY TO ESCAPE A LION
IS TO CLIMB A TREE

While not all lions climb trees, some lions can and do. Lions have been spotted (and photographed) perched on the limbs of trees at heights of up to 30 feet (9.1 m) off the ground. Why some lions climb trees is not known. It has been suggested that they do so to avoid the heat and the flies at the ground level.

THE LION IS THE KING OF BEASTS

The male lion is such a handsome, majestic-looking creature that it is little wonder he has become the symbol of royalty. But his appearance is deceptive. His behavior is far from kingly, or even gentlemanly.

1) The lion is not the strongest creature in his domain. If a lion met an elephant or a rhinoceros on a narrow path, he would be the first to move over. The lion is not even the largest of the cats; the Siberian tiger (unfortunately now almost extinct) is larger and stronger.

2) Lions fail to kill their prey quickly more often than cheetahs and leopards, which nearly always make quick, "clean" kills. Particularly when an older lion or a lioness hunts alone, without the aid of the rest of its family (called a pride), its first strike often does not bring down the zebra or large antelope, and it may be minutes before the suffering animal is killed.

3) The female does 90 per cent of the killing, but the male then shoves her aside and feeds first. Only after he has satisfied his hunger does he permit the lioness and the rest of the pride to feed.

4) Both male and female lions sometimes eat their own cubs.
5) The lion is sometimes as much a scavenger as a regal hunter. In some instances, lions get as much as half their food from carcasses killed by hyenas, wild dogs or disease.

Although he may not be king, the lion is a good survivor and not an endangered species.

THE GIANT PANDA IS A BEAR

The giant panda is as big as a bear and looks very much like one. It is flat-footed and walks on its soles like a bear. However, most scientists consider the giant panda to be a member of the raccoon family rather than a member of the bear family.

THE MOUNTAIN GOAT IS A GOAT

The mountain goat, or Rocky Mountain goat, lives in North America, from the Yukon to the U.S. Rockies. Although they resemble goats, these animals are not goats but goat-antelopes. Goats and goat-antelopes are related, however—both groups belong to the *Bovidae,* or cattle family.

THE HYENA IS A COWARD AND A SCAVENGER

The hyena is not entirely cowardly, nor is it only a scavenger. Although it feeds primarily on dead animals, it is also an active and aggressive hunter, feared by many (even larger) animals for its ferocity. They usually hunt in packs, but a single hyena can bring down a full-grown zebra. The hyena's jaws are among the most powerful in the animal world.

BEARS HIBERNATE IN WINTER

Some animals retire to underground shelters to pass the winter months when the weather is cold and food is scarce. The life processes are slowed down to the barest minimum to conserve energy and yet sustain life. When the woodchuck hibernates, for example, its body temperature drops drastically and its heart slows down to a pace of much fewer beats per minute. Hibernating animals are deeply unconscious.

What about bears? In spite of the commonly held view, bears are not true hibernators. Rather,

they sleep during the long winter months. None of their vital functions are significantly reduced. They can easily be awakened from their "hibernation" and will become fully active in a few minutes. However, it would not be a good idea to experiment with a sleeping bear, who might be rather grouchy if awakened from a cozy slumber.

BEARS HUG PEOPLE TO DEATH

An unarmed person attacked by a bear is in great danger, but will he be hugged to death? The "crushing embrace" or "deadly hug" of the bear is just a legend.

Bears injure and kill their victims with a mighty wallop of their forepaw. They also use their powerful teeth and their sharp claws. There is not a single instance on record of a person being hugged to death by a bear.

THE BUFFALO ROAMED NORTH AMERICA

The "American buffalo" is not a buffalo. It is a bison, which is related to the buffalo but does not quite qualify as one. The only true buffaloes are found in Africa and Asia.

THE KANGAROO IS THE
ONLY ANIMAL WITH A POUCH

A tiny baby peeking from the safety of its mother's pouch has come to be identified with the kangaroo, but at least 17 other marsupials (pouched mammals) exist, among them the koala, opossum, wombat, bandicoot, and even a species of mouse.

GOATS EAT TIN CANS

Because of its huge appetite, the goat has been accused of eating tin cans. Goats will lick the labels off tin cans for the salt content of the glue, and they nibble at almost anything out of curiosity, but they will not nor can they eat shoes, clothing or tin cans.

GORILLAS ARE BRUTAL ANIMALS

The gorilla is commonly thought to be a scaled-down version of King Kong, a beast that attacks without reason or warning. Nothing could be further from the truth. Actually the gorilla is a shy, withdrawn, moody animal that prefers to avoid dangerous encounters. It will not rush at an intruder unless it feels threatened and is unable to escape the situation. If an attack is provoked, it usually consists of a swipe with its powerful arm or a single bite, and then a quick retreat.

BULLS CHARGE ANYTHING RED

The color red is said to be irritating to a bull. The animal is thought to become especially enraged when a red object—a piece of cloth, for example—is moved about.

Actually, bulls cannot see colors. While not all animals have as yet been tested for color blindness, it seems that humans, apes and monkeys are the only mammals able to see colors.

If the bull does not become enraged at the sight of a red cloth, why is it used in bullfighting? The bullfighter, whether he is aware of it or not, is really waving a red cape around more to excite the audience than the bull. Human beings are very responsive to the color red. It is a bright color; it is the color of blood; it is a color associated with danger.

As for the bull, what excites him is not the color of the cloth, but its motion. Waving a green towel or a pair of yellow pajamas would excite him just about as much.

THE WOLF IS A FEROCIOUS ANIMAL

The wolf has long been thought to be an evil, ferocious killer by many people.

Recent scientific studies have shown that the wolf is not so ferocious, but a wary, often retiring animal with a complicated social organization. His strength is so limited, he cannot even overpower a deer without help, and prefers to attack only the weakest, oldest and sickest prey. Only occasionally does a wolf attack a lamb or calf, usually when no other food is available, although some individuals may make a habit of it. As for the notion that wolves are dangerous to humans, there is only one documented case of a wolf killing people, and that was in 1767!

WOLVES DO NOT BARK

Wolves are not supposed to bark, according to tradition, but only howl. The facts are otherwise.

The basic purpose of barking in dogs and wolves is to serve as an alarm or warning signal when an intruder approaches the den or living quarters. Howling, on the other hand, is a way animals separated by large distances contact each other.

Humans seldom get close enough to a wolf den to hear a wolf bark. Man is more likely to come into contact with wolves away from their dens. Wolves in the open howl because they are separated from each other while they are hunting. The case is otherwise with dogs. Humans are always invading the private domain of dogs. Barking is therefore heard frequently. Howling is less often heard because dogs are seldom separated from their masters for any length of time. Dogs can be made to howl, of course, by confining them beyond the reach of their masters.

Any differences between the vocal patterns of wolves and dogs may be explained on the basis of differences in the condition of their lives. The quality of howling may differ from dog to dog, but is basically similar to the long-drawn-out melodious sound of wolves.

Not only do the wolves bark, but so do their cousins, the foxes, jackals, and coyotes.

ACCORDING TO THE THEORY OF EVOLUTION, MAN DEVELOPED FROM THE APES

The theory of evolution developed by Charles Darwin (1809–1882) does not state that man developed from the apes. What the theory does say is that both man and the apes had a common ancestor. From this common ancestor, apes and man took separate evolutionary paths. One did not come from the other.

FLYING SQUIRRELS FLY

Flying squirrels have folds of skin between their front and hind legs. As the legs are extended sideways, each fold of skin is stretched into a flat surface, forming "wings" which enable the squirrel to take long, sailing leaps from one point in a tree to a lower one. Flying squirrels are really gliding, not flying, as their "wings" do not flap. Bats are the only mammals that actually fly.

RABBITS ARE SILENT ANIMALS

Rabbits seldom make a sound, true enough, but they are not voiceless. When in danger and particularly when seized by predators, they often emit loud, heart-rending screams.

While some animals do not use their voices frequently, biologists think that all higher animals can make some sort of sound.

THE RABBIT AND THE HARE ARE THE SAME

Although the rabbit and the hare are often thought to be identical, particularly in the United States, biologists use the names to refer to two different animals. Perhaps the most obvious difference between the two is the larger size of the hare, its ears and hind legs in particular. Rabbits, unlike hares, live in communal underground burrows, called warrens. The hare builds only a crude, simple nest on the ground and the young are born fully furred and with open eyes, whereas rabbits are born blind, hairless and helpless in a more elaborate underground nest. On the basis of these traits, the jackrabbit and snowshoe rabbit of North America are true hares, while the so-called Belgian hare is really a true rabbit. The cottontail, common in the eastern United States, does not fall neatly into either group but resembles the rabbit more than the hare.

PIGS ARE DIRTY ANIMALS

The pig's reputation as a dirty animal is undeserved. Before domestication, the pig was a forest-roaming animal. Today, confined by man in crowded, often dirty conditions—usually the worst part of the farm—the pig does what it can to remain clean.

True, pigs wallow in mud if they have the opportunity, but for excellent reasons. They cool off this way, and wallowing in mud serves to rid a pig's skin of parasites and diminishes the pain of insect bites.

Pigs are also said to be disgusting because they eat garbage, but usually that is what they are fed. Dogs, too, eat leftover human food, but we do not call the dog's eating habits disgusting.

Finally, pigs are said to be greedy. "To eat like a pig" means to stuff oneself. Wrong again! Pigs eat only as much as they need to satisfy their hunger, while cows and horses sometimes become very sick by overeating if allowed unlimited quantities of foods they like.

BEAVERS USE THEIR TAILS AS TROWELS

Children's books sometimes show beavers piling heaps of mud on their broad, flat tails and then using their tails as a plasterer uses a trowel to fill holes and cracks in their dams and lodges.

Beavers use their tails in a variety of ways. They use them as rudders in swimming and as props to support them when they sit on their haunches gnawing trees. A beaver also uses its tail to warn other beavers of danger, slapping it flat against the surface of the water to produce a loud splash. As for the notion that beavers use their tails as trowels, it is pure make-believe.

BEAVERS ARE EXPERT LUMBERMEN

Many stories are told of how the clever beaver can chew on a tree in such a way that it falls exactly where he wants it to fall. The fact is that the beaver will gnaw a tree on the side it can get to most easily and has no sense of where the tree will fall.

PORCUPINES SHOOT
THEIR QUILLS AT THEIR ENEMIES

It is not true that the porcupine, when harassed, shoots its quills at its adversary, but it's easy to see how this misconception got started. The porcupine usually defends itself with a sudden lash of its tail. Since its quills are loosely attached to its skin, if the tail misses its target some quills may fly out. Apart from this, the porcupine cannot throw or shoot its quills at its enemies.

The North American porcupine has as many as 30,000 quills, each about four inches (10.2 cm) long and tapered to a needle-sharp point. The surface of the quill is smooth except for an area just below the tip, where a band of tiny barbs is located. Each band has many barbs, which lie against the quill and point backwards along its shaft. When the quill is driven into the victim, the warmth and moisture of the flesh cause the tiny barbs to swell and become firmly anchored. Because the barbs are pointed backwards, the quill cannot be pulled out without also ripping some flesh out with it. The more the victim struggles to dislodge it, the deeper it penetrates, and if the quill pierces a vital organ the animal may die. Wolves, bears and mountain lions have been found dead with many porcupine quills embedded in their flesh.

ALL RODENTS ARE SMALL

Not so. The largest member of the rodent family, the capybara, is about four feet (1.2 m) in length and weighs as much as 150 pounds (68 kg). This animal lives near streams and rivers in Central and South America and swims expertly. Its jaws and teeth are extremely strong, able to cut through a metal bar.

MICE ARE QUIET

The phrase "quiet as a mouse" is inaccurate. Mice are far from silent. Investigators have found that in addition to squeaking, some mice make musical sounds similar to the twittering, chirping and warbling of small birds. Such noises are made by a variety of mice, including the common house mouse.

MICE ARE PARTICULARLY FOND OF CHEESE

Sorry, but all those cartoons that show mice gobbling up cheese as if it were their favorite food, are wrong. Mice do not prefer cheese and often will not touch it if any other food is available.

BATS ARE BLIND

The common expression "as blind as a bat" is simply not factual.

Bats are nocturnal; that is, they usually sleep during the day and are active at night. If disturbed and forced to leave their dark caves, they are only briefly inconvenienced. It takes the bat a while to adjust to the glare of daylight, but after that the eyes of bats are as good as those of many other animals.

BATS HAVE A BUILT-IN RADAR SYSTEM

How do bats find their way in the dark? Bats emit supersonic sounds—cries so high-pitched that the human ear cannot hear them. However, the bats can. The sounds are bounced off objects and are reflected back to the ears of the bat, telling the animal what objects are around it from moment to moment. This enables the bat to fly around without bumping into anything even in total darkness. A blindfolded bat, set loose in a dark room cross-strung with piano wires, can fly around at top speed and never touch a wire, but if its ears are plugged up, it blunders hopelessly because it cannot hear the guiding echo of its supersonic voice.

However, is this really a radar system? Radar bounces electromagnetic waves off objects to determine their location. The system used by the bat is based on sound; that is, it is a sonar system. The bat, then, uses a sonar rather than a radar system. Many people confuse the two.

VAMPIRE BATS SUCK BLOOD

The vampire bat makes delicate little nicks in the victim's skin and flesh with its sharp front teeth. The cuts resemble razor nicks rather than the two deep puncture holes usually shown in the movies. The vampire bat than laps up the blood like a kitten lapping cream. The vampire bat docs not and cannot suck blood.

Do vampire bats prefer human victims? As a matter of fact, they actually prefer cattle. However, they will victimize all kinds of animals, including man, if the opportunity presents itself and if they are hungry enough.

GIRAFFES HAVE MORE BONES
IN THEIR NECK THAN MAN

The neck of the giraffe is so long that people assume it has more bones than does the neck of man. This is not the case. Both man and giraffe actually have the same number of bones.

Even the smallest bird has more neck bones than the giraffe. The number of bones depends on the type of bird. Birds with longer necks generally have more bones. The English sparrow has 14, ducks 16, and swans 23. Both man and the giraffe have a mere seven.

A THOROUGHBRED HORSE
IS A HORSE WITH PURE LINES

One meaning of thoroughbred is an animal with pure lines. A thoroughbred dog, for example, is a dog of pure or unmixed stock. A Thoroughbred horse, however, is not simply a horse with pure lines.

The Thoroughbred horse was developed in England in the middle of the 18th century. In an effort to breed a fast horse, three English horses were paired with three horses from Turkey and Arabia. The resulting breed is known as the Thoroughbred. The Thoroughbred horse is not merely a horse with pure lines, as is commonly thought, but is actually a specific breed of horse.

WHITE HORSES ARE BORN WHITE

Other than genuine albino horses, ordinary white horses are not born white. Many horses born a certain shade, particularly dappled grey, become lighter and lighter as they grow older, until they become pure white. Such horses do not give birth to white colts, and white colts are practically unknown.

MONKEYS COMB THROUGH
EACH OTHER'S FUR FOR LICE OR FLEAS

Monkeys in zoos who search through the fur of other monkeys seem to be looking for fleas, lice or other insects. This is not so. Most monkeys in zoos are free of body insects, unless they are neglected or kept in dirty cages.

What the monkeys are looking for, and they will look for hours, are the tiny bits of salt from perspiration on the skin. When they find one of these salty morsels, they pop them into their mouths with great delight.

GROUNDHOGS CAN PREDICT THE WEATHER

This superstition is thought to have begun in Europe, where it was applied to the hedgehog. When the Pilgrims came to the New World, they brought this bit of folklore with them and applied it to the groundhog.

The groundhog, or woodchuck, hibernates in its burrow during the winter months. According to the superstition, the animal comes out if its burrow on the second day of February ("Groundhog Day") and looks around. If the sky is cloudy and the groundhog cannot see its shadow, it ends its hibernation and begins foraging for food. This is supposed to mean that the weather will be mild for the remainder of the winter. However, if the weather is clear and the sun is shining, the groundhog sees its shadow and scurries back into its burrow—a sure sign, according to the myth, that six more weeks of cold weather are ahead.

There is, of course, not one bit of evidence to support this belief. Why, then, do newspapers repeat the story about the groundhog year after year? Precisely because it is such a good story. Articles about cute little animals are always popular. Reports have even been known to poke sticks down the burrow of the woodchuck on February 2nd, to make it come out of its burrow so that its picture could be taken.

LEMMINGS PERIODICALLY MARCH TO THE SEA AND DROWN

The lemmings of Scandinavia are small rodents that are said to march in vast numbers to the sea, where they plunge into the water and commit mass suicide. This is believed to occur when their number exceeds the total that can be sustained by available food supplies. Scientists now consider such reports as legendary rather than factual.

The Scandinavian lemmings do migrate each autumn and spring in search of more plentiful food supplies. These migrations may involve millions of the small animals. Should they encounter lakes or streams, they make every effort to cross them. During such crossings, as one might expect, many lemmings may drown. Many more survive the crossings, however. Few, if any, lemmings reach the sea and drown. All the reports of mass drownings, curiously, are always about migrations said to have occurred long ago. No mass drownings have been observed by present-day scientists.

POLAR BEARS LIVE
IN THE POLAR REGIONS

Since polar bears are associated with ice and cold, it is commonly assumed that polar bears live both in the Arctic (northernmost) and in the Antarctic (southernmost) regions. Polar bears, in fact, live only in the Arctic. There are no polar bears in the Antarctic. Polar bears are really "North Pole" bears.

CATS ARE ONE OF THE
PRINCIPAL ENEMIES OF BIRDS

Cats admittedly stalk and kill birds. However, cats are responsible for only a tiny fraction of all bird deaths. Wildlife authorities insist that other birds kill far more birds than do cats. Jays, for example, are known killers of smaller birds, as are shrikes, hawks, owls, crows and magpies. Cats themselves, on the other hand, are the prey of some birds. The great horned owl, for example, attacks and feeds on cats.

It is simply not true that cats cause a serious reduction in bird population.

ALL CATS HAVE TAILS

Believed to have originated in the Far East, the Manx is one of the most unusual breeds of domestic cat. It has been bred for centuries on an island off the English coast in the Irish Sea, the Isle of Man. The Manx cat has two unique characteristics. For one thing, because the rear legs of the Manx are longer than its front legs, the Manx looks a bit like a rabbit when it moves. For another, the Manx is tailless.

In the majority of Manx cats, not only is there no tail, but there is actually a depression or hollow where the tail would normally grow. Any Manx cat born even with a tiny stump of a tail, which happens on occasion, is considered not true to the breed and is not eligible for competition in cat shows.

PURRING COMES FROM
THE VOCAL CHORDS OF THE CAT

Contrary to widespread belief, purring is not produced by the cat's vocal chords. How cats purr (or even why) is not fully understood. Some researchers think that purring is caused by a pulsating vibration of blood vessels near the trachea, or windpipe. Others believe that purring originates farther down the windpipe, in the lung or chest area. Still others consider purring to be merely the fluttering of the soft palate at the top of the throat. All agree, however, that purring is not made by the cat's vocal chords.

All healthy cats purr, whether they are big or small, wild or tame. A grown lion or tiger purrs as does the tiniest kitten.

THE PANTHER AND THE LEOPARD
ARE DIFFERENT ANIMALS

The names "panther" and "leopard" conjure up two very different animals—the first a black cat, the second a spotted one. However, leopard and panther are two names for the same animal. Further confusion arises from the fact that the term "panther" is often used in North America to refer to the cougar.

The leopard sometimes produces cubs with black coats. This is especially true of leopards in certain areas. Thus, the spotted and the black forms do not belong to different animals, but are simply two color phases of the same animal. The two colors can be represented in the same litter, and black and spotted animals can reproduce each other. If you look at a black leopard in the proper light, you can easily make out the spots.

ALL DOMESTIC CATS HATE WATER

Domestic cats are known for their positive loathing of water. One breed of domestic cat, however, is the exception to the rule. The Abyssinian cat loves water. A tawny brown or black, medium-sized, highly intelligent cat, the Abyssinian is of ancient lineage, for it is believed to be the sacred cat worshipped by ancient Egyptians. This cat breed enjoys dipping its paws in water and will play endless hours with dripping faucets.

NOT ALL DOGS ARE DESCENDED FROM THE WOLF

A number of the larger breeds of dog so resemble the wolf, it is easy to suppose that they are direct descendants of it. The German shepherd, the husky, the malamute come to mind. Other breeds, however, seem so far removed from the wolf it is difficult to imagine them in any sense related to the wolf. What do the chihuahua or the dachshund have to do with wolves? The ancestry of such dogs must have been along entirely different lines. Not so, say scientists. All dogs, no matter what breed, are direct descendants of the wolf. All dogs, in fact, are only domesticated wolves.

There are about 400 different breeds around the world. The large number of breeds and their variety is explained as the result of the dog's genetic variability. Unlike the cat, the dog is easily bred for specific characteristics. Thus the early Greeks developed dogs as sheep dogs, guard dogs, or as hunting dogs. The early Egyptians also bred dogs for specific traits.

No matter what the breed, however, and no matter how difficult it is to accept, all dogs are descended from the wolf. The next time your dog misbehaves, perhaps it is only the wolf in him acting up.

ALL DOGS BARK

All dogs do not bark. The basenji breed of Africa is a barkless dog.

The basenji is a medium-sized dog weighing 20 to 25 pounds (9 to 11 kg). It has a chestnut coat with occasional white spots, and a deeply wrinkled forehead which often gives it a somewhat amusing appearance. The basenji is an excellent hunting dog. One of the reasons it is used in hunting is that it is silent during the hunt. While the basenji never barks, it is not mute. It makes noises in its throat at times, especially when it is happy, but it does not manage a full bark.

One further peculiarity of the basenji is that it washes itself all over like a cat.

BIRDS

BIRDS HAVE SMALL BRAINS

A person with low intelligence is often said to be "bird-brained" because it is believed that birds have tiny brains. Actually, the brain of the bird is large and heavy in proportion to its body weight. Moreover, some birds—crows, for example—are quite intelligent.

BIRDS SING TO EXPRESS THEIR HAPPINESS

Human beings may sing out of happiness, but birds do not. Bird songs are actually part of a complex communication system that is used most during the breeding season.

A male bird sings primarily for two reasons: to announce that he has established for himself a territory that other males of his species should stay away from, and to attract a mate.

The females of most song bird species do not sing; a few do, but these do not sing as much as or as well as the males. The female canary, for example, has a weaker, shorter and less appealing song than the male.

Thus, bird song is an important part of courtship and related activity, not a method by which the bird announces its happiness to the world.

**BIRDS MUST FLAP THEIR WINGS
TO STAY IN THE AIR**

Condors, buzzards and hawks often fly at great heights and can remain aloft for hours on end without any movement of their wings. These birds are able to ride on rising air currents and take advantage of changes in air currents by slight motions of the body, head and tail. This kind of flight is similar to the flight of a kite, and is called soaring.

Certain birds of the vulture type depend so much on air currents in flying that they prefer to perch in trees on still, windless days when soaring would be too difficult.

ONE BIRD ALWAYS LEADS THE FLOCK

It is commonly assumed that one bird leads a flock of birds in flight. The leader is thought to be the oldest or the most experienced or the strongest of the birds. This is not the case.

Observe any flock of birds and you will note that the flock periodically breaks formation and reassembles a short distance beyond. Each time the flock does so, a different individual assumes the position at the head of the flock and becomes the new leader.

BIRDS CAN ONLY FLY FORWARD

Anyone who thinks that birds can only fly forwards has not seen the hummingbird in action. No other bird in the world can match the flying ability of this tiny bird. Hummingbirds can hover in one spot, move up, down, forward, backward and even sideways. How does the hummingbird do this? In addition to having an extremely rapid wing beat—as many as 75 beats a second—the hummingbird is able to rotate its wings at the socket during each beat. The wings of the hummingbird are like the blades of a helicopter, which change pitch as needed, making the helicopter extremely maneuverable.

ADULT BIRDS NEVER LOSE THE ABILITY TO FLY

After raising their young, most birds go through a period of moulting, shedding their feathers and growing new ones. They lose only a few feathers at a time from each wing, and new feathers quickly grow in to replace those lost. The bird is able to fly at all times.

It is not well known, however, that most waterfowl lose their ability to fly during moulting. Swans, geese, ducks and rails, among others, shed all their flight feathers at once. These birds may be totally incapable of flight for several weeks.

SLEEPING BIRDS SOMETIMES FALL FROM THEIR PERCHES

Impossible!

There are tendons in a bird's foot that extend from the toes past the ankle joint and up the leg to the muscles above. When a bird alights on a twig, its weight bends this joint and the tendons are stretched and pulled taut, which in turn makes the toes curl and grasp the perch firmly. Thus a bird is in no danger of losing its grip on its perch during sleep.

ALL BIRDS BUILD NESTS

No. Quite a few birds do not. Those birds which lay eggs on the ground often do not build nests. Many shore birds and terns merely scrape a slight hollow in the sand or grass into which they lay their eggs. Most parrots and many owls nest in tree holes that are lined with little or no nest material.

Some birds build no nests because they live as parasites on other birds. The cowbird, for example, lays its eggs in the nests of other birds, tricking other birds into rearing its young.

OSTRICHES BURY THEIR HEADS IN THE SAND

When an ostrich 8 feet (2.4 m) tall senses danger, it often drops down and stretches its long neck along the ground to make itself less visible, but it never buries its head in the sand. If the danger becomes threatening, the ostrich rises and runs away. It can attain speeds of up to 50 miles (80.5 km) per hour. It can also put up a pretty good fight. The ostrich is capable of inflicting serious wounds with its sharp toes and powerful kick. Men and even horses are reported to have been killed by the blows.

ONLY FEMALE BIRDS INCUBATE EGGS

Don't you believe it. Many kinds of brooding behavior may be observed among birds. In some, the female alone sits on the eggs. In others, the male does all the brooding; three examples of this are the rhea, kiwi and phalarope. In still others, both sexes take turns incubating the eggs. It has been estimated that in well over half of bird families both sexes share the task of incubation.

BIRDS DO NOT CARRY THEIR BABIES AROUND

A mother cat carrying her kittens from place to place is a common sight. If you said birds never do this sort of thing, you would be wrong.

An alarmed mother woodcock often tucks her chick between her thighs, clamps her legs together, and flies off to a safer place. A duck called the hooded merganser nests in tree holes that are sometimes high above the ground and some distance from water. When its ducklings are ready to leave the nest, it often carries them in its bill, one by one, to the nearest lake or marsh. Wood ducks have been observed doing this, too.

THE LOON IS A CRAZY BIRD

The expression "crazy as a loon" gives that bird a reputation that is undeserved. Although its call sounds crazy, the loon is actually one of the most intelligent birds.

BALD EAGLES ARE BALD

No, the bald eagle is not bald. This species of eagle, the symbol of the United States, has a dark head when young. As the eagle matures, the dark head feathers are replaced by white head feathers that extend over its neck.

All bald eagles are protected by law. However, many are shot every year simply because they make big targets for hunters. Pollution and insecticides are also killing this majestic bird. The number of bald eagles is decreasing and the species in danger of extinction.

"AS STRAIGHT AS THE CROW FLIES"

This is one of those common expressions which, when investigatcd, turn out to be misleading. Crows often do not fly in a straight line, preferring to meander widely or to follow a zigzag course.

PENGUINS ARE FOUND AT THE NORTH POLE

When people think of penguins, they think of funny little black-and-white creatures who live in cold, icy regions. Since the North Pole is cold, they assume the penguin lives there. They are wrong. The penguin lives in the Antarctic region, which includes the South Pole, as well as other parts of the Southern Hemisphere.

Similarly, many people think the polar bear lives at the South Pole. Actually, polar bears are found in the Arctic region, which includes the North Pole.

THE OWL IS WISE

The owl is a symbol of wisdom, but this is not accurate. Compared to many other birds, the owl is slow-witted and rather stupid.

THE PEACOCK DISPLAYS HIS TAIL

The beautiful fan of feathers you see is not the peacock's tail at all. These long, lovely display feathers (called a "train") grow on the lower part of the back, just above the true tail, which consists of 20 short, stiff, plain-colored feathers. When the peacock wishes to put on his display (to show off), the true tail lifts, fans out, and raises and supports the display feathers.

SCARECROWS FRIGHTEN BIRDS
BECAUSE THEY LOOK LIKE HUMAN BEINGS

It is popularly assumed that the human shape of scarecrows is what frightens off crows and other birds. However, it is not the resemblance to the shape of humans that scares the birds, but the smell. The scent of humans on the scarecrow's clothing is what frightens the birds off. After exposure to wind and rain, the clothing of the scarecrow loses its human smell and with it its effectiveness. A scarecrow that has been out in the open for any length of time may provide a decorative touch in your garden or field, but it will not rid you of crows or other birds.

BIRDS DO NOT FLY ANYWHERE NEAR AS HIGH AS AIRPLANES

While it is true that birds normally fly at heights below 3,000 feet (900 m), some bird species are able to attain altitudes which are generally associated only with airplanes.

Geese that migrate over the Himalaya Mountains have been known to attain 29,500 feet (9,000 m). One of the highest-flying birds known, the bearded vulture, reaches 25,000 feet (7,620 m). The mallard has been encountered at 21,000 feet (6,401 m). At these heights the air is so thin that man requires supplementary supplies of air merely to breathe, but the amount is apparently sufficient to sustain bird flight.

REPTILES AND AMPHIBIANS

THE DINOSAURS WERE UNSUCCESSFUL

Since the dinosaurs became extinct millions of years ago, it is commonly assumed that they disappeared because they were a failure as a life form. On the contrary, the dinosaurs were a highly successful group of reptiles.

Fossils of the first dinosaurs are found in the early Triassic period about 225,000,000 years ago. The last dinosaur fossils are found at the end of the Cretaceous period about 70,000,000 years ago. The dinosaur therefore lived for a period of about 150,000,000 years. This is a long time measured by any standard. Few life forms can equal the dinosaurs in duration of existence. Not only did they live a long time, but while they lived, they dominated the earth. Dinosaur remains have been found on every continent with the exception of Australia.

Why the dinosaurs became extinct is not fully agreed on. It is known that the disappearance of

the dinosaurs was not caused by epidemic disease, catastrophe, or by the destruction of dinosaur eggs by early mammal predators. One respected theory holds that dinosaurs succumbed to widespread and rapid changes in the geology and climate of the earth. However, if such changes were so dramatic, why did they affect the dinosaurs only and not other life forms as well? Curiously, not only did the dinosaur disappear at the end of the Cretaceous period about 75,000,000 years ago, but also the ichthyosaurs (swimming reptiles) and the pterosaurs (flying reptiles).

There are some who believe that dinosaurs never really disappeared in an evolutionary sense. According to this view, since it is believed that the dinosaurs gave rise to the birds, the birds are therefore feathered dinosaurs.

PREHISTORIC MAN AND DINOSAURS ONCE LIVED TOGETHER

Despite cartoon strips and television shows which sometimes depict man and dinosaurs co-existing, humans and dinosaurs could not have lived together.

Most estimates place the origin of man at 2–4 million years ago. The last of the dinosaurs disappeared more than 60 million years ago, at the end of the Mesozoic era. Hence, by the time man arrived on earth, the dinosaurs had been extinct for millions of years.

THE DINOSAUR WAS THE LARGEST CREATURE THAT HAS EVER LIVED

This may come as a surprise, but some dinosaurs were no larger than a chicken. Other dinosaurs, of course, were large indeed. *Brontosaurus* was over 60 feet (18 m) long and weighed between 30 and 40 tons (27 to 36 metric tons). *Diplodocus*, another dinosaur, had a length of up to 87 feet (26.5 m), but a weight of only 12 tons (10.8 metric tons). Most massive of the large dinosaurs was *Brachiosaurus*, which stood 40 feet (12 m) tall when it held its neck erect, was 80 feet (24 m) long and weighed 60 tons (54 metric tons).

However, none of these prehistoric creatures were anywhere near the size and weight of today's largest animal, the blue or sulphur-bottom whale. The blue whale may reach 110 feet (33.5 m) in length, and can weigh up to 175 tons (158 metric tons), the equivalent of 30 elephants and about three times the mass of the largest dinosaur.

SNAKES ARE SLIPPERY AND SLIMY

People who say that snakes are slippery and slimy have never touched one. The skin of a snake is cool, dry and remarkably clean. You will not see a dirty snake, either in the wild or in captivity. The reason is that the skin sheds water and mud and, being dry and smooth, does not readily pick up dirt.

SNAKE CHARMERS MAKE THE COBRA DANCE

Snake charmers claim they are able to put a snake, usually a cobra, into a trance. As the snake charmer plays his music, the cobra supposedly sways ("dances") to its rhythm and comes under the hypnotic power of the charmer.

Scientists doubt this is what really happens. The cobra is not hypnotized by the sound of the

music because, like all snakes, its hearing is extremely limited.

How, then, does the snake charmer make the cobra move as it does? Since snakes are very sensitive to vibrations, he may arouse the cobra and get it to rear its head by tapping his foot as he plays the music. Also, as the snake charmer and his flute move from side to side, the cobra is attracted by this and follows each movement intently. If the snake charmer did not move, the snake would not sway either.

The music, spoken commands and other antics of the snake charmer are really intended to charm the human spectators, not the snake.

THE BOA CONSTRICTOR KILLS BY CRUSHING ITS VICTIMS

The boa constrictor (and other constricting snakes) does not crush its victims to death. Instead, it quickly throws three or four coils around the animal it has caught and tightens its grip each time its prey exhales. Soon the victim cannot breathe and death follows. Rather than being crushed to death, the victim dies of suffocation.

ALL SNAKES ARE LAND CREATURES

Although the snake is thought of primarily as a land creature, there are some 60 true sea snakes. They live in the seas along the coasts of southern Asia, Australia, and as far as the east coat of Africa.

Sea snakes are well adapted to marine life. They are superb swimmers with flattened tails to aid their propulsion through water. Sea snakes, like other snakes, of course, just breathe air. They make efficient use of air, however. A single breath will last them an hour. For deeper dives, another system is used. Sea snakes swallow water, take oxygen from it, and then expel the water. They are able to stay under water for hours in this way. Sea snakes are wholly marine, giving birth at sea and dying if washed ashore, like whales, and unlike sea turtles and seals.

While only a small percentage of land snakes are poisonous, all sea snakes without exception are venomous. Any bite of a sea snake is a serious matter and can be fatal unless medical attention is provided immediately.

CROCODILE TEARS ARE FALSE TEARS

Crocodiles often do "shed crocodile tears" when feeding, but not out of mock pity for the victim they are devouring. The tears are simply an automatic reflex which occurs when they open their jaws wide, just as our eyes sometimes become watery when we yawn.

SNAKES SHED SKIN, HUMANS DO NOT

The shedding of skin is done not only by snakes, but by humans as well. Humans shed their skin partially when sunburned patches peel and when small flakes fall from the scalp as dandruff. Humans also shed their skins totally and this is normal.

The human skin consists of four layers. The top, or fourth layer, the *stratum corneum*, is constantly being shed from the body. No sooner do the cells of this top layer slough off into clothing or into the air than they are replaced by cells from the lower layers beneath. It takes about four weeks for a single cell to rise from the lowest or first layer to the top layer. Our entire skin, therefore, is replaced every 28 days.

The top layer, curiously, consists of dead cells. When we shake hands with each other, it is actually dead skin touching dead skin.

THE RATTLESNAKE ALWAYS WARNS
BEFORE IT STRIKES

Many snakes vibrate their tails when excited or threatened, but only the rattlesnake is equipped with a rattle. The tail of the rattlesnake usually vibrates about 48 cycles per second and may be heard up to a distance of 100 feet (30.5 m).

Can the rattlesnake always be counted on to rattle before it strikes, as many people suppose? No. Many victims have discovered, to their misfortune, that the rattlesnake may strike without the slightest warning. Furthermore, when a rattler does rattle, it is not a conscious attempt by the snake to warn an intruder, but simply the reaction of a nervous, angry rattlesnake.

Does the rattlesnake always take the time to coil before it strikes? Usually, but not always. The rattlesnake can strike without first coiling and often does when suddenly stepped on or otherwise surprised by a human or other animal.

THE CHAMELEON CHANGES COLOR TO MATCH ITS BACKGROUND

Chameleons do undergo rapid changes of color, but this has nothing to do with the color of their surroundings.

Cells in the chameleon's skin contain pigments that are involved in these color changes. When the chameleon becomes angry or frightened, nerve impulses sent to the color cells cause the colors to darken. Heat and cold, sunlight and darkness also affect the color of the chameleon.

Thus, temperature, light changes and the chameleon's state of mind are responsible for its color changes.

TOADS CAUSE WARTS

There is not the slightest evidence that toads cause or have anything at all to do with warts. Wart-like bumps on the body of the toad may resemble those on the human body, but medical scientists say that human warts are caused by a virus and are often associated with poor hygiene.

However, the skins of many toads are covered with a secretion that can cause irritation if it comes in contact with the eyes, mouth or a cut on the skin. These animals should therefore be handled cautiously.

FISH AND OTHER WATER ANIMALS

ALL FISH HAVE SCALES

Most, but not all, fish have scales. The catfish, for example, has no scales. Nor are fish born with scales. The scales sprout later, from under the skin. Does a fish grow more scales as it increases in size? No, the scales remain the same in number; each separate scale just grows larger.

FISH CAN'T DROWN

If "drowning" is taken to mean suffocation due to a lack of oxygen, then fish do drown.

Fish breathe by taking oxygen from the water. If the oxygen in the water is used up, the fish must either move to other waters where the oxygen supply is adequate, or die of suffocation. Millions of fish, in fact, die from suffocation each year. The problem is growing more serious as water pollution destroys oxygen supplies in a large part of the earth's waters.

FISH SWIM WITH THEIR FINS

The impression that fish swim with their fins is a common one, the result, perhaps, of observing how humans and other animals swim and assuming that fish swim in a similar way. Actually, fish propel themselves forward by moving their tails from side to side. The fins are used for steering and stabilizing.

ALL FISH LAY EGGS

A good many fish do not lay eggs but give birth to live young. Some of the fish that give birth to live young are oviparous, that is, the young are hatched from eggs retained within the body of the mother during development. Here there is no actual attachment to the mother through a placental connection, however. The eggs are merely stored within the mother's body until live birth takes place. Other fish are truly viviparous. Among the viviparous fish, the young are nourished through a placental connection as in the mammals. The true viviparous fish include moonfish, Mexican swordtails, surf fish, guppies, and the common minnow.

FISH IS BRAIN FOOD

Since fish is rich in phosphorus, and since the brain is also rich in phosphorus, the notion that fish is "brain food" is widely accepted. There is not the slightest evidence to support this notion.

Poultry, eggs, and milk are also rich in phosphorus. Are these not brain food equally? There is no reason to believe that the brain requires any special kind of nutriment. The brain's need for food is identical to that of any other part of the body. Fish is no more brain food than popcorn.

ALL FISH BREATHE WITH THEIR GILLS

All fish have gills, but some fish have lungs as well—four African and one South American species of lungfish, for example. These fish can survive for long periods out of water because their lungs are more developed than their gills. Some of these fish obtain up to 95 per cent of the oxygen they need from the air. In fact, some lungfish will drown if kept under water and not allowed to come to the surface to breathe.

During the dry seasons, the lungfish bury themselves in the mud of dried-up streams and lakes and secrete a thick mucous substance with which they encase themselves as though in a cocoon. They are able to remain buried in the mud, breathing oxygen for as long as 18 months, or until the next rainy season floods the area and the lungfish revive.

FISH BREATHE THE OXYGEN CONTAINED IN THE WATER MOLECULE

Many people are under the impression that the oxygen that fish breathe under water is the oxygen that is chemically united with hydrogen to form water. This belief is not without some logic since water, as we all know, is a compound that consists of one part oxygen and two parts hydrogen. Water is one of the most difficult of compounds to break down, however. To break water down into its two components requires complex chemical processes.

Exposed to the atmosphere, water absorbs air containing oxygen from it. The oxygen penetrates the surface and is dissolved into even the lowest part of the seas. It is this dissolved oxygen from the atmosphere, not the molecular content of water, that fish breathe. Fish breathe oxygen in water and not water itself.

FISH DIE OUT OF WATER

There are fish with the ability to remain out of water for long periods of time, and which can clumsily "walk" considerable distances. The walking catfish of Florida (originally from Thailand) are multiplying so rapidly that they are becoming a nuisance, and the climbing perch of India is well known. In other parts of the world, fish such as gobies, blennies and serpent-heads move through grass or mud from one body of water to another when necessary.

In addition to gills, all walking fish are equipped with breathing systems that enable them to take oxygen from the air. These fish "walk" awkwardly at best. The fins are used as legs, although they wriggle forward primarily by vigorous movements of their tails.

Some biologists believe that these fish are in the process of becoming land animals; that eventually, after slowly changing over a very long period of time, they will become adapted to living on land only and will not be able to swim like fish again.

FISH ARE SILENT

The whales, dolphins, and porpoises are mammals with developed vocal chords. It is hardly surprising, therefore, that these inhabitants of the sea are able to produce a number of sounds. Since fish lack vocal chords, one might assume they must be incapable of making sounds. This turns out not to be so.

Among the sounds produced by fish are croaks, grunts, coughs, whistles, and squeaks. Fish also make grinding, drumming, and rasping sounds. It is an uncommon fish that doesn't at least grunt. The most usual ways for fish to make sounds are by vibrating their swim bladders or by rubbing parts of their skeletons together. Some species snap their fins or gnash their teeth.

Little is known about the reasons why fish make sounds. The drumlike thumps of the drumfish and the groupers are thought to be defense mechanisms to frighten off approaching enemies. The "boat whistle" sound made by the toadfish may be related to the mating process. Other sounds are believed to warn the school of possible danger.

Far from being a world of silence, the ocean is a noisy place filled with a rich variety of sounds.

THE SHARK CAUSES MORE INJURIES TO MAN THAN ANY OTHER FISH

Not true. The stingrays, in fact, cause more injuries to man each year than all other species of fish combined. It is estimated that in the United States there are 1,000 cases of injury by stingrays each year. While the sting of the ray is usually not fatal, it can be extremely painful.

None of the various species of stingrays, which are related to the shark, are known to attack man. Almost every reported case of injury involved a victim who stepped on a stingray by mistake. Injuries have also resulted from attempts to handle these creatures.

Stingrays are mostly shallow-water creatures that often lie partially submerged under sand and mud. Because their flattened bodies are the same color as the bottom, they are difficult to see. The unsuspecting wader who steps on the ray is lashed by its tail, which is swiftly brought up and forward with great power. The tail not only cuts the victim, but injects poison into the wound.

Stingrays, when seen, should be left alone. One found in a swimming area can be made to move on by prodding it with a long pole (but never the hands or feet).

ALL SHARKS ARE DANGEROUS

Not all sharks are dangerous, any more than all snakes are poisonous. It is estimated that of the nearly 300 different sharks in the waters of the world, as few as 10 per cent are dangerous. The remainder are harmless and would much prefer to be left alone. Interestingly, the largest sharks are often the most harmless since they eat plankton rather than flesh. The largest shark, the whale shark, so-called because it resembles the baleen whale, may attain a length of 60 feet (18.3 m). This plankton eater is so gentle that divers may swim around it in perfect safety and even hitch a ride on its fin. The basking shark, 40 feet (12.2 m) in length, is also harmless.

Of course, if you are in the water and spot a shark, it would be the height of foolishness to hang around just to find out whether the shark is harmless or not.

SHARKS LOCATE VICTIMS THROUGH THE SMELL OF BLOOD

Sharks react strongly to the smell of blood in water. However, it is not primarily through the smell of blood that sharks locate victims. A shark is able to sense vibrations in water by means of delicate hairs along the sides of its body. The splashing of a swimmer is conveyed quickly from distances far beyond the shark's range of smell.

It is these vibrations rather than the smell of blood that generally attract sharks to humans in the water. More than half of known shark attacks have occurred in water five feet (1.5 m) deep or less, and nearly all the victims were not bleeding before the attack. As far back as ancient Roman times, attacks on people without wounds have been reported.

However, should a shark, or rather a number of sharks, pick up the smell of blood, a gruesome spectacle the likes of which are not to be found anywhere else in nature may ensue. When a number of sharks close in on a bleeding victim, they go into a feeding frenzy. They bite and tear at almost anything, including themselves, as well as the victim.

PORPOISES PERFORM BRILLIANTLY IN WATER SHOWS

Almost all the trained "porpoises" that entertain audiences at water shows are not porpoises at all, but dolphins. Usually, bottle-nosed dolphins are used for this purpose.

The dolphin is one of nature's most intelligent animals. These friendly, playful mammals are genuinely fond of human beings, and can be trained to imitate human speech to some extent. They are known to rescue one of their group that is injured or sick, supporting it at the surface so that it can breathe. There have also been reports of dolphins saving the lives of drowning persons by pushing them to shore. It is not known whether the animal is being consciously helpful or only playful in doing so.

The shark is the dolphin's main enemy. A shark is either evaded with great speed and tricky maneuvering or, if encountered by a school of dolphins, battered to death with the dolphins' hard noses.

THE OCTOPUS SQUEEZES ITS VICTIM TO DEATH

Under no circumstances does the octopus strangle or crush its victims with its arms. The arms (tentacles) are used solely for holding the victim so that it can be bitten by the parrot-like beak of the octopus. Many octopus species are venomous, injecting poisonous saliva into the wound made by the beak. So far as is known, however, only one octopus, the small blue-ringed octopus found off Australia, is capable of killing humans.

A large octopus may look threatening but is seldom a real danger. Octopuses (octopi) are shy and prefer to hide in the safety of rocks and crevices, escaping the notice of their enemies by an amazing ability to change color and blend in with their surroundings.

The many tales of giant octopuses attacking men and boats are just fantasy. If there is any foundation to such stories, it is the giant squid and not the octopus that is probably involved. The giant squid is not only larger than the octopus, it is also a more aggressive creature. Specimens of giant squid have reached 55 feet (17 m) and weighed over 4,000 pounds (1,812 kg).

HORSESHOE CRABS ARE CRABS

Horseshoe crabs are not crabs; they are not even crustaceans. That is, horseshoe crabs, despite their appearance, are not closely related to such water creatures as the shrimp, crab, lobster and crayfish. Horseshoe crabs, instead, are related to the arachnids. The nearest relatives of the horseshoe crab are such creatures as the mite, tick, scorpion and spider.

Horseshoe crabs are called "living fossils," and with good reason. They evolved 150 million years ago, and have not changed since then.

FLYING FISH REALLY FLY

Glide, yes; fly, no. The idea that these fish "flap their wings" in true flight is wrong. The enlarged pectoral fins of an airborne flying fish remain rigid, and thus the flying fish cannot be said to fly like birds.

This is not to deny the remarkable ability of the flying fish to take to the air. When pursued by larger fish, it uses its powerful tail to build up enough speed in the water and then takes off, gliding as far as 200 yards (183 m) in the air before dropping back into the sea.

THE SHELLS OF CRABS ON THE BEACH
ARE THE REMAINS OF DEAD CRABS

One can usually find the shells of crabs on the beach. It might be supposed that these shells are the remains of dead crabs. This is erroneous.

The shell of the crab serves as an external skeleton. It is inflexible and cannot grow. As the crab grows, the animal finds the shell too cramped. The crab must shed its outer covering the way a snake discards its skin.

The shells of crabs seen on the beach are generally shells cast off or moulted during growth rather than the remains of dead crabs. The same applies to the shells of horseshoe crabs also frequently seen on beaches.

BARNACLES ARE MOLLUSCS

Barnacles cling to rocks, piers and ship bottoms. They look very much like small clams. In spite of their appearance, however, barnacles are not mollusks. Barnacles are true crustaceans and are related not to the clam or to the oyster, but to the lobster, the crab and the shrimp.

Young barnacles resemble other young crustaceans and swim freely through the water. After a short time, however, the young barnacles select a spot in which to settle down. The spot selected is of great importance, since, once attached to a surface, the barnacle never moves again.

The barnacle secretes a cement which permanently anchors it to the selected spot. The barnacle then produces a quantity of lime which eventually encloses the animal in what resembles a clam shell. The barnacle inside, lying on its back with its neck stuck tight to the anchored spot, points its feet upward. When the shell opens, as it does periodically to feed, the feet fan the water thus pulling in particles of food. A freely moving creature in early life, the barnacle adopts a life of total immobility as an adult.

INSECTS, SPIDERS AND RELATED CREATURES

INSECTS HAVE RED BLOOD

No, the red blood you may see on a squashed insect, such as a mosquito, is actually blood the insect has sucked from a red-blooded animal. The greenish color of the squashed bodies of other insects is from the undigested vegetable matter in the digestive tract. Insect blood is colorless, or faintly yellow.

DRAGONFLIES ARE DANGEROUS

For some unknown reason, the dragonfly with its huge transparent wings is thought to sting. It has no stingers and is in all ways completely harmless. These interesting insects fly with great speed and have the unusual ability to dart backwards and forwards without turning. On the whole they are beneficial to man, feeding on mosquitoes, gnats and other small insects which they capture and devour while in flight.

INSECTS USE THEIR ANTENNAE FOR FEELING

Insects often seem to be exploring their environment when they wave their antennae about. It appears to us as if the insect is feeling its way along. Actually, the antennae of the insect are primarily organs of smell and not of feeling.

TAPEWORMS MAKE PEOPLE EAT A LOT

It is commonly believed that the presence of tapeworms in the intestinal tract will result in an insatiable appetite. "You must have a tapeworm," is often said to a person who has an endless need for food. Actually, the food needed to maintain a tapeworm is negligible. People infested with tapeworms do not need or desire any unusual quantities of food.

THE WINGS OF BUTTERFLIES ARE COLORED

Not exactly. The wings of butterflies have no color. All those beautiful colors and designs are produced by thousands of tiny colored scales on the surfaces of the wings. If the wings of butterflies (and moths) are touched when the insects are handled, these scales fall off very easily, revealing a transparent wing underneath.

THE PRAYING MANTIS IS PROTECTED
BY UNITED STATES LAW

Because the praying mantis is so beneficial to man, it is commonly believed that this insect is protected by law. It is not. Currently, no insect species is protected by U.S. law.

THE CATERPILLAR IS A KIND OF INSECT

The caterpillar is not a kind of insect but a stage in the development of an insect. The caterpillar is the larval form of the butterfly or moth. That is, the caterpillar is the stage before the insect turns into a butterfly or moth. The caterpillar does not mate. It cannot because it has not reached adulthood. Only butterflies and moths are able to mate.

THE CLOTHES MOTH EATS WOOL

A moth known as the "clothes moth" is commonly believed to eat holes in clothing, furs and even carpets. However, the moth itself is not responsible for such damage.

The moth eats nothing at all. It exists solely for the purpose of forming and depositing eggs. The eggs then hatch into larvae—a stage in the insect's development in which it resembles a small worm or caterpillar—and it is these larvae that eat holes in the clothing. The larvae later develop into moths and the cycle is repeated.

Do moth balls help? Yes, they keep adult moths away. However, they do not kill eggs or larvae already present. Storage of clothes in cedar chests also helps to protect them against damage by moth larvae.

ALL MOSQUITOES LIVE ON BLOOD

The males don't! They lack the proper mouth parts for piercing animal skin and sucking blood. Only the female mosquito eats blood. When it is unable to obtain animal blood, the female, like the male, feeds on plant juices, nectar and fruit.

ALL INSECTS EAT AND DRINK

Not so. Among many insects the larvae do all the eating and drinking, the adults none. The adult mouth-parts of such insects become so degenerated that they are all but useless for feeding and drinking. The adults survive on the nourishment gathered during the larval stage.

Adult insects that neither eat nor drink include the mayflies, midges, and the emperor moth. The latter is especially surprising since the emperor moth is one of the largest of moths and may attain a wingspread of a foot (30 cm).

THE SILKWORM IS A WORM

The silkworm is not a worm. It is actually the larva of the moth *Bombyx mori*. Silk is made from the cocoon which encloses the larva.

MOTHS AND BUTTERFLIES GROW

Not at all. When we look at small and large butterflies, it is only natural to suppose that these represent old and young individuals. This is not the case.

Moths and butterflies do not appear in their winged form until they have reached the final phase of their development. When they have reached the winged stage, they do no more growing, any more than do adult humans.

THE MOSQUITO'S BITE
CAUSES SWELLING AND ITCHING

The bite of the mosquito is followed by swelling and itching. It is not the bite itself that causes the itching or the swelling, however.

The mosquito feeds on blood. Animal blood being too thick to be sucked up by the mosquito, the victim's blood must be thinned out first. To accomplish this, the mosquito injects a saliva-like substance into the victim which acts to thin out the blood.

The bite itself is seldom felt. The puncture in the skin is so small, there is hardly any pain, and most people are not aware of being bitten at the time. The swelling and itching experienced after the bite are not due to the bite itself, but to the presence of the saliva of the mosquito in the victim's bloodstream. The swelling and itching are an allergic reaction to a foreign substance. It is not the result of the skin being punctured.

THE COMMON HOUSEFLY BITES

The housefly cannot bite or chew anything. Its mouth parts are soft and fleshy, designed for sucking liquids only. However, the stable fly, which is similar in appearance and also visits human dwellings, has mouth parts formed especially for piercing flesh. Other biting flies include horseflies, deerflies and black flies.

To eat, the common horsefly first deposits some liquid from a previous meal to dissolve the food it wishes to dine on, a lump of sugar let us say, then sucks up the resulting sweet liquid.

MOSQUITOES PREFER HUMAN BEINGS

Mosquitoes must prefer to dine on humans. Why else would they bite us so often? Tests show that mosquitoes, if they have a choice, really prefer to feed on horses, cattle, pigs, and dogs.

Some humans seem to attract mosquitoes more than others. Mosquitoes prefer children to adults, fair people to dark ones. Although mosquitoes do not generally range far from their breeding sites, they have been known to travel up to 30 miles (48.3 km) in search of a steady supply of victims—non-humans preferably.

THE TARANTULA IS DANGEROUS TO MAN

Death from the bite of a giant tarantula is extremely rare.

The tarantula may look dangerous, but it is basically sluggish, easily tamed and seldom bites humans. There are many species of tarantula, some with bodies 3 inches (7.6 cm) long and 10 inches (25 cm) across with legs extended. Their bite is painful but has little other effect on man; a bee sting may hurt more and is frequently more dangerous.

THE SPIDER IS AN INSECT

The spider may look like an insect, but it is not one. The spider belongs to a group of creatures called arachnids.

How do spiders differ from insects? An insect has three pairs of legs; the spider has four pairs. An insect body is divided into three parts—the head, the thorax or middle part, and the abdomen at the rear—while the body of the spider is divided into two parts, the head and thorax being joined. Growing out of the head of an insect are two sense organs called antennae; spiders have no antennae. Spiders have simple eyes, often eight in number, whereas insects have several simple eyes and two compound eyes made up of many little facets for more effective sight. An insect breathes by means of small holes along its body called spiracles and air tubes called tracheae; a spider's breathing apparatus consists of many leaf-like plates called book lungs. Finally, spiders have no wings, while insects usually have two pairs.

The closest relatives of the spiders are the scorpions, ticks and mites, not the insects.

SPIDER WEBS ARE DELICATE

The thread spun by the spider may look weak, but actually spider's silk is stronger for its size than any other fiber found in nature. It is very elastic, stretching one-fifth of its length without breaking. The tensile strength of spider silk is greater than that of steel.

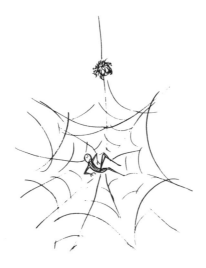

A CENTIPEDE HAS A HUNDRED LEGS

Sorry, but the common house centipede (*centi-* meaning one hundred) has 30 legs. Garden centipedes have 21 pairs of legs. Furthermore, there are others with well over 100 legs.

Does the millipede (*milli-* meaning one thousand) have a thousand legs? No. The maximum number of legs is slightly more than 200, and most common millipedes have only 30 to 60 pairs of legs.

Index